PERCEPTRON

Before you start to read this book, take this moment to think about making a donation to punctum books, an independent non-profit press,

@ https://punctumbooks.com/support/

If you're reading the e-book, you can click on the image below to go directly to our donations site. Any amount, no matter the size, is appreciated and will help us to keep our ship of fools afloat. Contributions from dedicated readers will also help us to keep our commons open and to cultivate new work that can't find a welcoming port elsewhere. Our adventure is not possible without your support.

Vive la Open Access.

Fig. 1. Detail from Hieronymus Bosch, *Ship of Fools* (1490–1500)

First published in 2025 by dead letter office, BABEL Working Group, an imprint of punctum books, Earth, Milky Way.
https://punctumbooks.com

The BABEL Working Group is a collective and desiring-assemblage of scholar–vagabonds with no leaders or followers, no top and no bottom, and only a middle. BABEL roams and stalks the ruins of the post-historical university as a multiplicity, a pack, looking for other roaming packs with which to cohabit and build temporary shelters for intellectual vagabonds. BABEL is an experiment in ephemerality. Find us if you can.

ISBN-13: 978-1-68571-216-7 (paperbound)
ISBN-13: 978-1-68571-217-4 (PDF)
ISBN-13: 978-1-68571-298-3 (EPUB)

DOI: 10.53288/0408.1.00

LCCN: 2025948625
Library of Congress Cataloging Data is available from the Library of Congress

Editing: Eileen A. Fradenburg Joy and SAJ
Book design: Hatim Eujayl
Cover image: Photograph of Frank Rosenblatt's July 31, 1969, United States of America passport. In Box 18, Folder Miscellany, 1965–1971, undated. Library of Congress. Maurice Rosenblatt papers, 1910–2003 (bulk 1942–2000), Box II:18, Part II: Frank Rosenblatt Papers, 1943–1971. Library of Congress, Washington, DC. Fair Use.
Cover design: Vincent W.J. van Gerven Oei

punctumbooks
spontaneous acts of scholarly combustion
DLO

HIC SVNT MONSTRA

PERCEPTRON

James E. Dobson
Rena J. Mosteirin

Contents

Contents

Acknowledgments

The research for this book required the support and effort of many individuals. We are grateful to Lewis Wyman, reference librarian at the Library of Congress, for his assistance in locating and scanning archival materials. Frank Rosenblatt touched the lives of many people during his short life but left little of his voice to archival record. We are grateful to Philippa Claude, Virginia "Ginny" Miller, A. Amasa Miller, and Eugene "Gene" Endres for spending hours talking with us about their experiences in the Chateau Rosenblatt community and for sharing their memories of Frank Rosenblatt. Gene died not long after our interview, in October 2022, and we are thankful for his generosity and support of this project. William "Bill" Mutch not only consented to an interview to discuss his many recollections of Rosenblatt and the wide circle of people around Rosenblatt but also provided documents, including a list of residents of Chateau Rosenblatt and most importantly, he gave us access and permission to share the photographs that he had taken of Rosenblatt and his many friends during the 1960s and 1970s. Bill also gave us photographs from Rosenblatt's own camera. These images document major events in Rosenblatt's life and career and hint at his rich private life. They give a fuller picture of him as not only a brilliant scientist but also as a living human, with a wide range of interests and a caring sensibility. These images add immense value to our exploration of the Perceptron, Frank Rosenblatt, and this incredible moment in the history of computing and machine learning. We are thankful to Bill for sharing these important and touching images and for sharing his many memories with us. Finally, thank you to punctum books for your unflagging advocacy for open access and the centering of experimental work. Thank you, especially, to Eileen and Vincent for your support and care for all your authors and for our project.

PART ONE

FRANK IN LOVE

in duplicating
determining how human
learning operates

a better learning
the behavior of networks
study of signal

Similar to those
biological neurons
but not better

Well, first of all let me say that we are interested in duplicating human learning, if it is possible to do so. We are interested in determining the extent to which it is feasible to consider such a thing as duplicating human learning, or at least understanding how human learning operates. Whether or not there exists a better mode of learning is in a sense an empirical question to which I don't feel we can supply an answer at this point.... We are interested, however, not only in studying human learning, but in studying the behavior of networks which include biological nervous systems as a subclass. This is to say, we are interested in the study of signal transmission networks which involve connected nodes or cell points which have functional characteristics similar to those of biological neurons, but not necessarily better.

— Frank Rosenblatt, 1960, in response to a question about the Perceptron

Brilliant Offspring

Dr. Rosenblatt picked up a silver cream pitcher beside his coffee cup. "I recognize this as a pitcher, though I've never seen it before," he said.

In these matters, you know, use follows invention.

What, we asked, *wasn't* the perceptron capable of?

Dr. Rosenblatt threw up his hands. "Love," he said. "Hope. Despair. Human nature, in short. If we don't understand the human sex drive, why should we expect a machine to?"

New Navy Device Learns by Doing

embryo electronic
computer today
walk, talk, see, write

The Weather Bureau
$2,000,000
right and left

build the first thinking machine
as the human brain
as do human beings

recognize people
call out their names
conscious of their existence

The perceptron
like
the human

Device Expected to 'Think'

first true robot able
only in science-fiction stories
weapon in the arsenal
the USSR may explore

ability to follow instructions
to do mathematical computations
nonbiological system held to
a mosaic of photocells

form generalizations, and discover
output cable to a printer
display and control
though still unborn

Dr. Frank Rosenblatt
"theory of statistical separability"
International Business Machines 704
Dr. Rosenblatt lies

the recognition is direct
through his eyes
still in the future
the great breakthroughs of the human brain

Shades of Frankenstein!

The Navy is well
important defense of the Western World

Naval Research proved a robot
would have original ideas

gleaned from outer space
distinguishing between

airplanes missiles
bombers fighter planes

responding to verbal commands
unearthing of information buried in library books

distinguishing between
Wagner Mozart
beagle hound collie dog

the robot has yet to be built
human eye certain brain

Dr. Frank Rosenblatt
staged a demonstration

For Machines

almost like the human mind
electronic brains
punched cards, perforated tape
make decisions, sort objects
learn a language by the Berlitz method

The system was set up to sort —
nothing more
it was not told

Those with squares on the left half of the card
    were distinguished from those with squares on the right half

If it could make four choices
whichever the Perceptron thought the most logical way
the difference between Collies and Beagles

large parts of it are destroyed

a serious mistake

almost fantastic to conjure with

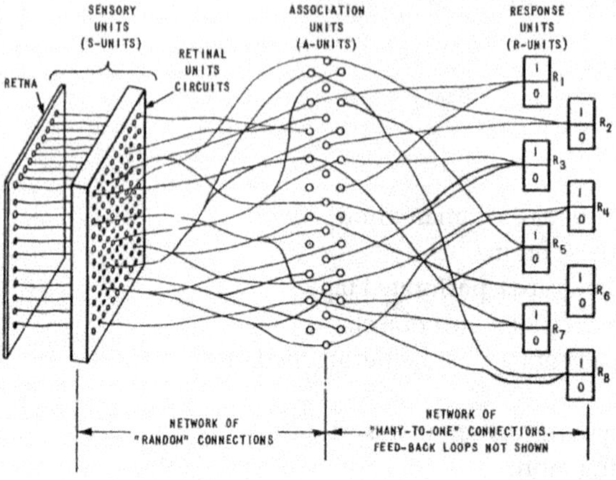

Fig. 1.1. Diagram of the Mark I Perceptron. In John C. Hay et al., "MARK I Perceptron Operators' Manual (Project PARA)." Fair Use. https://apps.dtic.mil/sti/tr/pdf/AD0236965.pdf.

Feed me sensory units
Split the data into two A-units

R1 is either a 1 or a 0
R2 is either a 1 or a 0

Everything I can see is either a 1 or a 0

The Automation of Photointerpretation (using a 3x3 pixel matrix)

To the automatic
To surveillance
To reconnaissance

To the segments
To the mechanisms
To boundaries

To military goals
To blobs* and ribbons
To encoded relations

*blobs are marked for additional analysis

A brain model or pattern recognition device?

Frankenstein monster or Navy Robot?

important military target or photographic artifact?

target location or background object?

military goal or noise?

the human brain or the Perceptron?

B.F. Skinner's Questions

> How could a person anticipate and hence prepare for what another person would do?... How can a mental event cause or be caused by a physical one?... Why explain the explanation?... What would you do about war, or population, or pollution, or racial discrimination, or the revolt of the young?
>
> — B.F. Skinner, from *About Behaviorism*

How could a pesticide anticipate and hence prepare for what another pesticide would do?... How can a mental evolution cave or be caused by a piano?... Why explain the explosive?... What would you do about a warbler, or porch, or poltergeist, or racial disguise, or the revolver of the young?...

What would you do about a warder, or porpoise, or polygon,... What would you do about a warhead, or portent, or polytechnic,... What would you do about warmth, or a portfolio, or pomegranates, or racial disillusion, or the rhinoceros of the young?

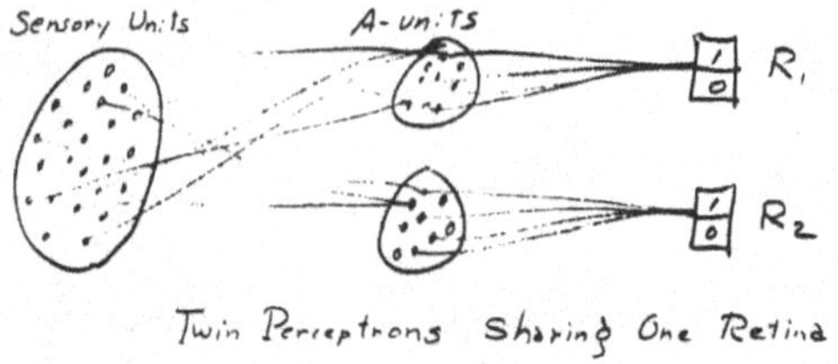

Fig. 1.2. Drawing of the design for Twin Perceptrons. Albert E. Murray, "Perceptron Applicability to Photointerpretation," Phase 1 report for Project PICS, Report VE-1446G-1, 1960. Fair Use.

If the machine can see, then consider Frankenstein.
What are we looking at here? The first neural network.

The Perceptron may acquire a stronger or weaker voice
based on who speaks for it.

Random Connections.
Many-to-One Connections.

Feed-back loops not shown.
Flop-over threshold.

If it does what it says, then the machine can see...
I don't understand what I'm seeing here.

The org chart helps me not at all.
Is it a monster or isn't it?

Rosenblatt proposed using three different sets of simplified McCulloch-Pitts neurons to create his initial neural net. These sets of simplified neurons were known as the S, A, and R units. The S units made up the sensory system and were imagined as the 20x20 "point" retinal mosaic. The A units were association units, which summed the activation values from the S units, which would be connected to some number of different A units. The connections would be either positive, "excitatory" connections, or negative, "inhibitory" connections. The A units would in turn be connected to a smaller number of R or response units. These were activated by some number of A units reaching a pre-defined threshold value.

Sense

Association Association
Association Association

Response
Response

[Sense] Points of Black on a White Background

[Association] wild turkeys in a field of snow
  [Association] speckled white chocolate
    [Association] words on a page
      [Association] colony of penguins on an iceberg

[Response "excitatory"] before the war

[Response "inhibitory"] after the war

Points of White on a Black Background

Snow falling in dark forests
pearls sewn onto a black velvet cape
stars infinite against the universe
shake of powdered sugar on a chocolate cake
white spots on a black cat
polka dots on a dress a lit city
drops of white paint on asphalt
white birds flying over the sea
a river running with little leaping fish catching silver shards of moonlight

it's coming for me

sweeter and sweeter

A Straight Line

Trail of a jet
architectural edge
where the road abides
mast rising true from a sailboat
new antenna
power lines the spine of a book
pine tree

bubbles going up

(too close to) the edge

this is the only way
what's left when the rubble is cleared

A Curved Line

rainbow road turns
a smiling cheek
a domed cake pine trees in a hurricane
horns mountain ridge

wave claws curly hair

sails curved with wind leaping humpback whales

these dreamy days after a storm
this is where we come to pray

Frank Rosenblatt

July 11, 1928
July 11, 1971
psychologist head of
director of
Neurobiology and
his Perceptron
models of brain function
and an ability to learn

the transfer of learned behavior
from rats by the injection of brain extracts

a new technique to detect the presence of stellar satellites

music

liberal politics

in a series of Vietnam protest activities in Washington
constructive aspects of the upheavals in spring 1969

This willingness to help us all.

Frank Rosenblatt

died on a Sunday afternoon in Chesapeake Bay.
Associate professor
exceptionally broad
brain function
electronic device which was
biological
developed and extended
Principles of Neurodynamics

He also had a new stellar technique
and music, which he composed
his special contribution

to political statistics in New Hampshire
and California
in New York State
in Washington

At Cornell a deep interest in student affairs
which led him to help very many
who had difficulties in adjusting

This willingness
we have lost

Frank Rosenblatt

boating accident
he was
then went

Systems Research
Behavior within
Department of

and simultaneously
with models
extensive in astronomy

computer techniques
McCarthy primary
Democratic reform

Vietnam protest
He had his relationships
and his brilliant mind

Notes on the Perceptron Form

The Perceptron Form is a new poetic form that mimics the logics of early machine learning. It's essentially an erasure poem that samples from two different sources, offering divergent readings. For "Poem in the Perceptron Form," I used lines from Rosenblatt's *New York Times* obituary as the source for stanzas one and three. An article about Rosenblatt from *The New Yorker,* published on December 6, 1958, served as the source text for the lines in stanzas two and four. Visualize it like so:

Stanza 1: Obituary
Stanza 2: Article
Stanza 3: Obituary
Stanza 4: Article

Within the stanzas themselves, the logic organizing the lines alternates deliberately between two different ways to read Rosenblatt's life. The first line and the one-stanza lines represent the weight statement. The poem mimics learning as described by Rosenblatt, separating the two readings,

Line 1: Reading A
Line 2: Reading B
Line 3: Reading A
Line 4: Reading B,

and combining them somewhat randomly in the weight statement:

(word from Line 1, word from Line 2, word from Line 3, word from Line 4).

The weight statements that follow the original weight statement are assembled by taking one word from each line in the stanza that precedes it. The weight statement that originates the poem — in this case, “Dr. Frank Rosenblatt died” — signals the reason for writing the poem in the first place.

Poem in the Perceptron Form

Dr. Frank Rosenblatt died

died here yesterday in a boating accident
one aspect dealt with models of brain function
it was his 43rd birthday
at his death he was acting chairman

Boating function birthday death

My colleague disapproves of all the loose talk one hears
    nowadays about mechanical brains
Dr. Rosenblatt picked up a silver cream pitcher beside
    his coffee cup
Of what practical use, we asked, would the perceptron be?
Biologists claim that only biological systems

Disapproves Dr. Rosenblatt perceptron claim

the scientist was born July 11, 1928
research interests were broad with models of brain function
he is survived by a sister and a brother
a new method for the detection of satellites

Scientist broad survived by satellites

Hope. Despair. Human nature, in short.
a brief exegesis of their brilliant offspring
I recognize this as a pitcher though I've never seen it before
Rosenblatt threw up his hands

Human offspring recognize hands

Unfashionable Machines

In Memory of Frank Rosenblatt

Rigorous work does not make the perceptron look very good
A youthful wave of optimism
Perceptron researchers applied their unfashionable ideas
The pendulum swung back toward learning machines in the mid-1980s

Rigorous youthful unfashionable machines

In a boating accident in Chesapeake Bay
his Perceptron, which showed an ability to learn
Research psychologist, senior psychologist, head of cognitive systems
in numerous papers and a book, *Principles of Neurodynamics*

Accident device systems numerous

This story seems to call for a plea of guilty or innocent:
Three decades later, machine learning is a thriving research field.
Did Minsky and I try to kill
Cell phones recognize speech Automobiles are driving themselves

Guilty decades Minsky recognize

music, which he composed, and liberal politics
to help very many who had difficulties
a series of Vietnam protest activities in Washington
This willingness to help was a feature of all his relationships.

Composed help protest help

A Promising Line of Research

Whereas humans can learn how to perform

a task, computers must be programmed.
The only scientific way is to prove it mathematically
programming is laborious and error prone
Funding was no longer forthcoming.

Must prove error forthcoming

He lived in Brooktondale, N.Y., an Ithaca suburb
The instrument was an electromechanical device
Son of Dr. Frank Rosenblatt and Katherine Rose Rosenblatt
trained rats by the injection of brain extracts

Lived device son rats

somehow protected from these events by the iron curtain,
Perceptrons interrupted a promising line of research
successes of the multilayer perceptron
    back-propagation algorithm
progress had already come to a virtual halt

Somehow interrupted perceptron progress

Mrs. Bernice Evans of New York, and Maurice of Washington
memorial service will be held at Cornell in Ithaca
in brain mechanisms and in models
in New Rochelle, N.Y.   in Buffalo

of New York held models in

Principles of Neurodynamics vs. Perceptrons 0.0

It is only after much hesitation

Neurodynamic cybernetics bionics
How is the Perceptron performing today?
autonomics biomimesis synnoetics
And how are Neuron and Electron behaving?

Bionics today autonomics are

The simplest learning machines
parallel computation, pattern recognition
one cannot think productively about such matters
knowledge representation and learning

Simplest recognition such learning

Intelectronics robotics perceptron
The aims are in need of clarification
theoretical nerve nets
the admitted lack of mathematical rigor in preliminary reports

Intelectronics need nets mathematical

Progress has been so slow
Some readers may be shocked
little of significance changed since 1969
has not there been a revolution?

Slow readers little revolution

Principles of Neurodynamics vs. Perceptrons 0.1

A perceptron is first and foremost a brain model

for the emergence of various psychological properties
simplifications have been made from biological systems
in a serious study of neurodynamics
these principles may be freely applied

Emergence from study may

A perceptron is a device capable of computing
diameter-limited perceptrons gamba perceptrons
we present here a simple example of a theorem
order-restricted perceptrons random perceptrons

Capable diameter here random

Principles, motivations and accomplishments of perceptron
the writer is convinced
a consistent theoretical position
the student would be well advised

Accomplishments convinced consistent student

Bounded perceptrons contain an infinite number of
proof requires us to consider just four figures
concerned neither with "learning" nor probability
this proof shows that perceptrons cannot recognize

Bounded figures "learning" cannot

Principles of Neurodynamics vs. Perceptrons 0.2

Seductive aspects of Perceptrons

The purest vision of the perceptron
"programming" takes on a pleasingly homogenous form
this procedure is guaranteed
"programs" people have been tempted to call learning

Purest pleasingly procedure tempted

characterized by the great freedom
Because of a common heritage in the philosophy
reliance placed on acquired biases
The writer makes no claim

Freedom philosophy biases claim

To separate reality from wishful thinking
ease and uniformity of programming have been bought at a cost!
any physically real perceptron has a limited repertoire
realistically measure this cost

Reality cost repertoire cost

never studied in isolation
the writer's predilection for a probabilistic approach
not concerned with a single perceptron
is shared with such theorists as Minsky, among others

Studied probabilistic concerned Minsky

Principles of Neurodynamics vs. Perceptrons 0.3

On the one hand / on the other hand

the brain operates by built-in algorithmic methods
the brain operates by non-algorithmic methods
analogous to those employed in digital computers
bearing little resemblance to logic and mathematics

Brain operates those little

even within a simple combinatorial subject such as this
in Chapter Six we obtain a series of positive results
our intuition is still weak in the field of computation
at such astronomical rates as to be physically meaningless

Subject series weak physically

the brain is a conventional computing mechanism
the performance required from his model
adaptive processes play a non-essential role
the system is required to normalize and compare

Brain model adaptive system

machine could retrace its steps in the course of exploring
here the situation is much simpler
the maze of possible paths through a figure
there are surely many more surprises to come

Exploring simpler paths there

Principles of Neurodynamics vs. Perceptrons 0.4

One should be cautious about using "intuition" here

Note that we did not allow reflections, yet
by a suitable tolerance theory
these reflectionally opposite figures are now confused!
could presumably be made consistent

Not suitable confused presumably

complicated problems (e.g., those involving "insight")
on learning and retention of nonsense
problem-solving behavior appears to depend upon
using himself as a subject

Complicated nonsense upon himself

the threshold conditions are sharp
especially if there is any problem of noise
coefficient sizes are often fatally large
even with simple square-root noise

Threshold of fatally simple

to find actual physiological memory
electrical stimulation on the cortex
memory may involve modification of the connections
with hallucinatory clarity

Actual electrical memory clarity

Principles of Neurodynamics vs. Perceptrons 0.5

Concluding Remarks

the provision of "eyes and ears" for automata
the "heuristic program" approach to psychological functioning
shared sensory experience, can "comprehend"
goal-motivated behavior becomes the main object of study

Automata approach sensory behavior

we possess such *small* degrees of consciousness
networks cannot perform useful matching functions
so little insight into the nature of our own machinery
we certainly do not mean to suggest that

Such functions nature certainly

present environment and state of neurodynamic theory
on the other hand, the memory problem remains paramount
as perceptron models become more sophisticated
"biological maturity" must await the solution

State memory sophisticated solution

perceptron invented by Frank Rosenblatt in a single act
This is an oversimplification
the final proof vindicating his insight
reflective thought is the lesser part of what our minds do

Invented this his mind

Frank and Rod Visit Morocco

Fig. 1.3. Rod Miller. Image from Frank Rosenblatt's camera, courtesy of William Mutch.

"Frank was in love with my brother Rod"

(imagined) Postcard from Morocco

When I wake up, it's like
I'm still dreaming. Looking
closely at Rod, I know one day I will
carve his face in stone. I want to make
something from his deep beauty,
something that will last forever.

Fig. 1.4. Rod Miller. Image from Frank Rosenblatt's camera, courtesy of William Mutch.

"Frank was in love with my brother Rod."

(imagined) Postcard from Morocco 2

We left campus! We
left that world. Now the days
blow light through our hair.

Fig. 1.5. Rod Miller. Image from Frank Rosenblatt's camera, courtesy of William Mutch.

"Frank was in love with my brother Rod"

(imagined) Postcard from Morocco 3

Let's do what we do.
Let's never go home.
Together we are the bluest sky.
No poet can paint
what we have done.

Fig. 1.6. Rod Miller. Image from Frank Rosenblatt's camera, courtesy of William Mutch.

"Frank was in love with my brother Rod"

(imagined) Postcard from Morocco 4

Every single arch here is
a shell-eyed door that never blinks.
These doors are not doors at all
nothing ever closes. Rod stares in wonder
at the space between where we stand
and everything else in this world.

Frank in Spain

Fig. 1.7. Frank Rosenblatt. Image from Frank Rosenblatt's camera, courtesy of William Mutch.

(imagined) Postcard from Spain

I no longer defend myself
against the sweetness of flowers.
I know what they say, "Frank is a character!"
Sunlight filters through the leaves.
You would turn me into a poet.

PART TWO

BRILLIANT OFFSPRING

Courage is to smile
When the doctor jabs the needle
Into frightened flesh, thinking
(But not saying) "Look, Mother,
How brave I am!"
Courage is to see dreams crumble,
And then shaking out the dust,
To dream again; to apprehend
The ambush hidden in the path
And still go forward; to explore
Within the hidden craters
Of your own desires; to submit
The working and creations of your mind
For public judgment.
And courage
Is to hope
When others have surrendered.
And courage
Is to face surrender
When others hope.

—Frank Rosenblatt, "Courage"

Introduction: An Invention and an Inventor

"Courage is to see dreams crumble, / And then shaking out the dust, / To dream again," writes Frank Rosenblatt, an American psychologist and early computer researcher, in an unpublished poem titled "Courage." Rosenblatt's poem, his only work of creative writing in the archival record, was read by Father David Connor, Cornell University's Catholic chaplain, at a memorial for Rosenblatt following his early and tragic death, the result of a boating accident on his forty-third birthday. Rosenblatt had been swept overboard while sailing with two of his young friends on *Shearwater,* his recently purchased sloop.

Rosenblatt was attempting to cross Maryland's Chesapeake Bay. They had just set sail from Oxford, on the eastern shore, and were heading toward Annapolis. Pulled overboard and brought back aboard with some struggle, Rosenblatt's youthful crew attempted to keep him alive, but he succumbed before the Coast Guard arrived, their delay partially the result of communication complications involving *Shearwater's* marine radio.

By the time of the accident, Frank Rosenblatt, who had just a few years earlier been the subject of numerous newspaper and magazine features and the celebrated instigator of an exciting new field of research, had disappeared almost entirely from public consciousness. Despite the near ubiquity of artificial intelligence and machine learning in contemporary culture, little is known today about the mid-twentieth century moment in which these technologies were invented or about the short life and dreams of one of the most important and brilliant contributors to their development. While the uneven successes of machine learning over the past seventy or so years have continually forced these technologies as well as their inventors and proponents to numerous scenes of public judgment, Rosenblatt's legacy and memory have likewise been shaped by his identity, by his politics, sexuality, and family history.

Rosenblatt's short poem at the beginning of this section is about resilience. It imagines the emotional difficulties that a highly creative person might experience in depending upon the public's recognition and reception of the "working and creations of your mind." This poem might strike one as an odd choice for a eulogy. Despite or perhaps even because of the consigned tone — the poem's resilience is not pollyannish but a measured and self-assured pragmatism — "Courage" provided Father Connor with a fitting statement to summarize Rosenblatt's rather mercurial life and academic career.

This short poem is one of the few pieces of personal writing left by Rosenblatt, certainly the only one to appear in print. "Courage" was printed in the stately *Congressional Record* because it was recited at Rosenblatt's memorial. US Representative Hugh L. Carey of New York presented his own tribute to Rosenblatt at the US House of Representatives on Wednesday, July 28, 1971, a short seventeen days after Rosenblatt's untimely death. Carey's remarks were more than the recognition of an important scientist, they were a gesture of condolence to Rosenblatt's older brother, Maurice, whom Carey invoked in his comments as "one who, in the tradition of that family, a great New York family, has worked very earnestly to improve politics in our country, and therefore to improve our country through better politics."[1]

In his presentation of materials to be included in the *Congressional Record,* Carey also included a tribute from Senator Eugene McCarthy, who had spoken at Rosenblatt's memorial at the invitation of Maurice Rosenblatt. McCarthy referred to Frank Rosenblatt as "a kind of universal brother, brother to the members of his family, to the members of the faculty who knew him, to the students who have spoken here, and I think in a sense to all of us."[2] The author of "Courage" was certainly familiar with the vicissitudes of a research career performed mostly in public and the necessity of embracing both hope and surrender. To the many individuals within his large social circle, however, Frank Rosenblatt was primarily known as a source of steadfast support to those in need.

In the years immediately preceding his death, Rosenblatt worked across widely diverse fields — from studying the effects of LSD on laboratory rats to developing novel planet detection methods in astronomy — with outright failure, seemingly, especially from the perspective of university administrators, to be the only connection found among these many projects. By 1971, the year of his death, almost every one of Rosenblatt's varied endeavors and interests had been understood by his peers to have crumbled into dust, with several of his projects — most notably his search for extraterrestrial species with radio telescopes

1 Hugh L. Carey, quoted in U.S. Congress, House, *Congressional Record,* Vol. 117, part 21, July 28, 1971, 27716, https://www.congress.gov/92/crecb/1971/07/28/GPO-CRECB-1971-pt21-3-2.pdf. For an account of Maurice Rosenblatt's political activities, including his co-founding of the National Committee for an Effective Congress in 1948 with Eleanor Roosevelt, see Shelby Scates, *Maurice Rosenblatt and the Fall of Joseph McCarthy* (University of Washington Press, 2006).

2 Eugene McCarthy, quoted in U.S. Congress, House, *Congressional Record,* vol. 117, part 21, July 28, 1971, 27718, https://www.congress.gov/92/crecb/1971/07/28/GPO-CRECB-1971-pt21-3-2.pdf.

and his efforts to extract and implant acquired knowledge in rats—becoming highly visible and very public failures. Yet his major work, an invention known as the Perceptron, has now come back from the dust to claim its rightful place as the origin story of the most cutting edge and wildly successful contemporary computing technologies of the twenty-first century.

The deep neural networks powering popular chatbots and breakthroughs in science and medicine today (and also at the core of today's most insidious financial instruments and surveillance technologies) are directly descended from Rosenblatt's Perceptron, which was also seen as his most public failure during his lifetime.[3] Contemporary uses of the phrase "artificial intelligence" refer mostly to what is called Generative AI (GenAI), especially in the form of interactive chatbots. These chatbots are built on top of predictive Large Language Models (LLMs) constructed from incredibly large and dense neural networks. While much larger than the networks used by Rosenblatt and implementing recently created features, these LLMs are at their core the same technologies developed by Rosenblatt in the 1950s. These tools came to general awareness when OpenAI made publicly available their GenAI-based chatbot that they called ChatGPT in November of 2022.

ChatGPT is an application. The underlying LLM takes its name from a series of OpenAI-created models called Generative Pre-trained Transformers, or GPTs. The transformer is a relatively recent neural network architecture that learns contextual information from massive samples of data. These have been applied to images and especially to text. Transformers are classed as "deep learning" because they are organized in layers. The largest LLMs are constructed from networks with billions

3 In this book, we capitalize "Perceptron" and use the term to refer to the abstract algorithm, the software machine. Some invocations of Perceptron used in this book will also refer to the hardware implementation of the algorithm, a physical computing machine, what would become known as the "Mark I," but "Perceptron" throughout this book will name Frank Rosenblatt's abstract computational model, whether implemented as a machine, in hardware, or simulated in software.

or perhaps even a trillion or more parameters organized into a hierarchical and layered structure.[4] While a transformer's major innovation is the encoding of contextual information, which means that the neural network learns something about the sequencing of words or pixels from the position of supplied inputs, in its basic operation it closely resembles the networks constructed by Frank Rosenblatt in the late 1950s. While requiring a tremendous amount more computation and training data, Rosenblatt certainly could have imagined contemporary versions of artificial intelligence and chatbot applications.

Frank Rosenblatt did not live to see the rebirth and success of his early vision and dream, but he lived his life with the type of courage required to make his longest-held and most wild hope possible: the creation of a machine, inspired by the brain's complex network of neurons, that could learn to distinguish between visual patterns sensed from its environment. In tracing the connections among his varied interests and from the knowledge that his invention would come to be one of the most valuable and dazzling contemporary technologies, Rosenblatt's research focus seems less random. In almost all of his activities, Rosenblatt was motivated by an investigation into the operation of the transfer of learning. He was interested in learning, in whether it was accumulated and transferred, stored, or if it was produced collectively through the lateral sharing of acquired experience.

While neural networks, machine learning, and artificial intelligence seem like utterly contemporary twenty-first-century technologies and ideas, these were in fact all born in the middle of the twentieth century, shortly after the conclusion of World War II. These technologies were created in a milieu shaped by the intersections of mid-century scientific research and the newly created digital and analog computing systems. This ad-

4 The canonical reference for the network architecture of transformers is Ashish Vaswani et al., "Attention Is All You Need," *Advances in Neural Information Processing Systems* 30 (arXiv, 2017). For more background on this architecture, see James E. Dobson, "On Reading and Interpreting Black Box Deep Neural Networks," *International Journal of Digital Humanities* 5 (2023): 431–49.

mixture was transformative and would come to alter all of these fields. For media historian Orit Halpern, neural networks and machine learning were "the technological manifestation of a more widespread reconfiguration and reorganization of human subjectivity, physiology, psychology, and economy."[5] These same technologies produced new accounts of the brain and mind that would result in additional reconfigurations of these scientific fields.

Neural networks enable broad interdisciplinary thinking, as Ranjodh Singh-Dhaliwal, Théo Lepage-Richer, and Lucy Suchman argue: "Through their rhetorical deployment of neural tropes, neural networks promote a vision of data extraction and pattern recognition as functions constitutive of the brain itself, advancing a form of recursive thinking about computer and machine intelligence that goes beyond mere analogies and metaphors."[6] In taking up the genealogy and the ongoing development of these networks through a reconstruction and interpretation of the life of their most important early researcher, this book hopes to bring the animating concepts and thoughts invoked by Singh-Dhaliwal, Lepage-Richer, and Suchman into a richer historical and cultural context. By reading these ideas through the lens of an intellectual biography, previously obscured connections between various knowledge fields and culture and between politics and practice are made more visible and analyzable.

Driving these transformations, especially in the United States, were government imperatives to create new command and control technologies that would produce and process intelligence from both domestic and foreign sources. The early origin story of today's most influential and debated technologies locates these innovations at the intersection of several areas of mid-twentieth-century scientific and military research. Con-

5 Orit Halpern, "The Future Will Not Be Calculated: Neural Nets, Neoliberalism, and Reactionary Politics," *Critical Inquiry* 48, no. 2 (2022): 336.

6 Ranjodh Singh-Dhaliwal, Théo Lepage-Richer, and Lucy Suchman, "Introduction: Rendering the Neural Network," in *Neural Networks*, ed. Ranjodh Singh-Dhaliwal et al. (meson press, 2024), 5.

cerned with automating highly skilled and risky activities like landing aircraft and the labor-intensive interpretation of aerial reconnaissance images, the United States military and Department of Defense turned to recently emerging technologies from the intersection of psychological and engineering research and redirected the efforts of laboratories and universities to these problems. It was the Cold War-era funding priorities of the Department of Defense, more than any other force or desire, that shaped the early development of machine learning and created the conditions that made the invention of the Perceptron possible.

The dearth of reference to Rosenblatt in the early histories of machine learning and artificial intelligence is due to reasons both personal and impersonal. Matteo Pasquinelli's *The Eye of the Master: A Social History of Artificial Intelligence* is one of a few recent academic histories that revisits and reconsiders Rosenblatt's legacy. In his introduction, Pasquinelli lays out the stakes of his project and the prominent role played by Rosenblatt. Pasquinelli's social history offers, in his words, "a more compelling history of AI about which, especially regarding Rosenblatt's work, critical and exhaustive literature is still missing."[7] Given the media and scholarly attention to Rosenblatt during the 1950s and early 1960s, how did he become erased from the history of artificial intelligence and machine learning?

To some degree this was inevitable, as Rosenblatt's name was unavoidably linked to a particular program or branch of artificial intelligence. This branch was rooted in neural networks and what was referred to as "connectionism" in the 1980s and 1990s. Today these are recognized as the most likely line of research and product development related to machine learning. In the 1980s and 1990s, while these technologies were continuing to be developed and expanded and even finding productive applications, they were mostly regarded as a dead-end. Another branch of artificial intelligence was known as symbolic AI. If the

7 Matteo Pasquinelli, *The Eye of the Master: A Social History of Artificial Intelligence* (Verso, 2023), 15.

theory organizing connectionism said that knowledge could be acquired by neural networks that began from nothing—initialized with all zeros—symbolic AI forwarded the idea that knowledge needed to be categorized and organized by human experts in order for artificial intelligence to succeed. Symbolic AI implemented rule-based systems for processing and evaluating knowledge, such as complex decision trees that encoded decision-making criteria. From the tragic end of Rosenblatt's life until the advent of neural language models, symbolic AI, for the most part, was perceived as the only path forward for building complex knowledge systems. During these in-between years, Yann LeCun implemented new versions of Convolutional Neural Networks (CNNs) that leveraged some of the same innovations added to networks by Rosenblatt. These CNNs bested benchmarks and were used for a number of computer vision tasks, especially for character and letter recognition and most famously for zip code detection by the US Postal Service. During this period, David E. Rumelhart, Geoffrey E. Hinton, and Ronald J. William rediscovered and made practical Rosenblatt's theoretical conception of "back-propagating error correction," which he had sketched out in his *Principles of Neurodynamics* (1962). Despite these impressive achievements and developments, neural networks in this moment were still thought of as impractical as well as an inferior technology to symbolic or what philosopher John Haugeland termed Good Old-Fashioned AI (GOFAI).[8]

Pamela McCorduck's *Machines Who Think: A Personal Inquiry into the History and Prospects of Artificial Intelligence* (1979) was one of the first histories of artificial intelligence.[9] Its early publication date meant that this book would come to define and shape public perception about the field and set the stage for much of the historical work that would follow. At the begin-

8 GOFAI is coined in John Haugeland, *Artificial Intelligence: The Very Idea* (MIT Press, 1985).

9 Pamela McCorduck, *Machines Who Think: A Personal Inquiry into the History and Prospects of Artificial Intelligence*, 2nd ed. (AK Peters, 2004).

ning of the scant two pages that mention Rosenblatt in *Machines Who Think,* McCorduck quotes an unnamed scientist who had called Rosenblatt "a real medicine man" and a "press agent's dream."[10] Dismissing his work as mere showmanship rather than a serious intellectual contribution to AI research, McCorduck adopts the attitudes of the symbolic branch of artificial intelligence. While Rosenblatt's Mark I Perceptron has been recognized by the Smithsonian Museum as an important contribution to American science and technology, *Machines Who Think* seeks to erase the machine and the man from this history. McCorduck figures Rosenblatt as an irritation within the early AI scene, something that needs to be removed to remove the discomfort caused by his presence. She takes this term, "irritant," from one of her sources and repeats it several times; for example:

> Case Western's Leon Harmon, who worked on the von Neumann machine at the Institute for Advanced Study at Princeton, and who describes himself as perhaps the first computer operator, still seethes about walking into the Smithsonian and discovering that beside the von Neumann machine, which well deserved to be there, stood a Perceptron, sharing floor space as if it were equally important. Harmon doubts that we'll ever learn much about brain operation from studying electronic hardware, and believes that the really interesting and potent things the computer in our head does are inscrutable. If he was once enamored of the work Grey Walter and W. Ross Ashby were doing, it's an infatuation he's outgrown. Rosenblatt only irritated him.[11]

McCorduck transforms this scene of Harmon "seething" as he walks through the Smithsonian into an outright dismissal of Rosenblatt. She seems surprised that some computer scientists do not share this attitude. She describes their sense of Rosen-

10 McCorduck, *Machines Who Think,* 105.
11 Ibid.

blatt's legacy in terms more personal than technical, returning to the idea that he was a showman and his research was driven by the force of his personality: "Rosenblatt also influenced a number of people at the Stanford Research Institute who still speak respectfully and affectionately of him. But his Perceptron ran into both practical and theoretical difficulties, and Rosenblatt's accidental death seemed to rob the effort of its energy to continue."[12]

Understanding neural networks as poor and ineffective simulations of the brain, McCorduck makes the claim that symbolic AI was preferrable to neural network-based models because of the way in which information is represented within the networks. Without the ability to link a set of input values to a specific set of activated neurons, she and the AI researchers she references believed that these models could only provide an inferior form of knowledge representation:

> One problem with a Perceptron was that it could classify stimuli it received but it lacked an internal representation of that act. Therefore, it couldn't refer in some symbolic way to the act of perception, but had to recapitulate the act itself exactly, which put it in the position of being no better off when repeating the act again. Symbolic representation, by which machines (and humans) deal with a host of phenomena without having to reiterate them in their totality, is central to intelligent behavior, to memory, and to consciousness.[13]

McCorduck's history, as she herself admits in her subtitle, was a personal history. It was shaped by her personal access to informants and sources—most importantly, those researchers employed by Carnegie Mellon University, including Allen Newell and Herbert Simon, frequent references cited by McCorduck with much authority. *Machines Who Think* was not the only

12 Ibid., 106.
13 Ibid.

account of the early development of artificial intelligence and Rosenblatt was not the only figure erased and dismissed from this history, but McCorduck's dismissal of Rosenblatt is glaring.

In reading the life of Frank Rosenblatt alongside the development of the Perceptron, associations turn into important pathways through which we can better understand how the mid-twentieth century lives on in twenty-first-century computing technologies. This book, therefore, recounts the history of both an invention and an inventor. The Perceptron is a simple but powerful algorithm that was first formally described in 1957.[14] It was originally dreamed up by Rosenblatt as a new kind of a computer that would be modeled on the brain and visual perception systems. Rosenblatt imagined that this device would become an alternative to conventional digital computers. It would be easier to use and operate and it would provide a mechanical laboratory through which psychologists would come to understand the operation of the human brain.

The Perceptron's futuristic name was derived from the language of 1950s science fiction and technology marketing. Based on the latest scientific and philosophical accounts of the organization of the human brain and its visual system, its name gestures toward an imaginary automaton equipped with a machinic mode of vision and perception — the yet-to-be-named technology of computer vision.[15] The perceived success and limitations of the Perceptron, as well as the legacy of its inventor, would determine the reception of neural networks, machine learning, and artificial intelligence for both the scientific community and the general public for many decades to come.

Rosenblatt first imagined the Perceptron as a design for both a physical computing machine and a machine-independent al-

---

14 Frank Rosenblatt, "The Perceptron: A Perceiving and Recognizing Automaton (Project PARA)," Report 85-460-1 (Cornell Aeronautical Laboratory, 1957). The majority of the CAL reports for Project PARA can be found in the HathiTrust Digital Library, scanned by Cornell University.

15 On the history of computer vision and the Perceptron's role in the development of these technologies, see James E. Dobson, *The Birth of Computer Vision* (University of Minnesota Press, 2023).

gorithm. In his initial proposal, Rosenblatt explained that this alternative to early digital computers, which were cumbersome to program and inefficient for many tasks, would be self-organizing and capable of programming itself. It would do so through a limited set of repeatable instructions that Rosenblatt argued would always result in a solution, if one was possible. The Perceptron was thus imagined as both a machine and an algorithm. While it was developed under the government funding-friendly code name of "Project PARA," an acronym for the "*P*erceiving *A*nd *R*ecognizing *A*utomaton," the Perceptron was neither an automaton nor was it even initially implemented as a piece of physical computing hardware. It was an idea. The Perceptron was the formal articulation of a statistical model based on early- and mid-twentieth-century neurophysiological theories of perception and brain function.

As an abstract model, the Perceptron could be turned into software as a series of instructions or embedded in specialized hardware. Like many twentieth-century technological innovations, it was modular and could be simplified or made more complex through the addition of new features and components and even multiple versions of itself. The Perceptron was first implemented on a digital computer as a simulation of an analog machine before it could be implemented as the physical machine of Rosenblatt's imagination. Due to the speed and flexibility of general-purpose digital computers, it would be the fate of the Perceptron and neural network technology in general to remain simulations.

The Perceptron took several different forms during its early years and continues to live on in the present, transformed in response to changing conditions, much like the biological organs which served as its inspiration. The Perceptron appeared during a transitional moment in several scientific fields, most importantly in the field of psychology. Psychology was undergoing a transition as new cognitive theories had come along to displace those that had previously dominated the field. Behaviorism, the study of behavior and learning, was replaced with the experimental study of human cognition. This shift was also accompanied by the greater use of computation and modeling in the analysis of experimental data. Rosenblatt's research straddled both sides of these transitions as he studied human learning using a cognitive model derived from physiological research. Computers and data-driven research were central to Rosenblatt's research and even in his earliest psychological research he made use of novel methods and designed his own processing hardware. Rosenblatt also made use of comparative studies drawn from animal research. In turn, the cognitive paradigm that led to a revolution in psychology and the invention of the field of cognitive neuroscience would come to adopt Rosenblatt's approach of modeling human mental processes with neural networks.

The environment that shaped the Perceptron and made its creation possible was saturated with the thinking and language of this moment. It was also a product of US Cold War science. Funded by the military and national science and defense organizations, the Perceptron emerged from the laboratory as a prospective tool in both the imaginary and real battles and conflicts with other nations. The Cold War period had an overriding cultural logic of its own — a binary logic that operated alongside and sometimes was embedded within inventions like the Perceptron and other advanced technologies of the moment.

Frank Rosenblatt invented, or as he would have put it, "discovered" the Perceptron algorithm and method and served as its primary promoter, fundraiser, and chief publicist. This invention provided a platform for simulating and testing a whole set of concepts and theories related to Rosenblatt's career-long interests in learning, parenting, training, knowledge transfer, and perception. Both Rosenblatt's career and reputation were attached to the Perceptron. It was his legacy and his most important contribution to science, yet it would not be his only project, nor would it come to define how he thought of himself as a researcher.

In Rosenblatt's lifetime, the Perceptron would come to be perceived by many as unworkable, a failure. It was understood to be an interesting research project, but wildly oversold. Who precisely had oversold the Perceptron is not exactly clear. Rosenblatt had an interest in science fiction and an active imagination and would sometimes offer speculative predictions about the future capabilities of machines and technologies like the Perceptron. He would later comment that the press reported on his invention with "all of the exuberance and sense of discretion of a pack of happy bloodhounds."[16] Rosenblatt's invention found an eager audience of funding agency staff, reporters, and the wider public, who saw science and technology as both a frontier to be conquered and a battlefield to be won. The Cold War and the so-called "space race" had produced a competitive and deeply nationalistic drive to develop new technologies that could demonstrate the power and scientific cunning of the United States.[17]

Rosenblatt was attracted to big problems, problems that seemed insurmountable to other researchers and that were not answerable through a single perspective or field. He liked complex ideas and solutions that crossed boundaries and fields of expertise. Throughout his short career, Rosenblatt would take up big problems that were well beyond his area of specialization and his training as a psychologist. It was perhaps his experience with scientific programming and designing early computer systems that best enabled him to search for solutions to such a wide range of problems: in describing big problems and rendering them computable, he was able to collect and process data from many different domains. Rosenblatt had unwavering faith in his ability to examine and analyze data originating in environments as varied as animal experiments, human vision, speech recognition, and the detection of planetary objects in space.

The parental metaphor is an overused cliché. It is routinely used to describe inventors and scientists. Too frequently, in naming an individual the "father" or "mother" of an idea or device, attention is taken away from the constellation of people

16 Frank Rosenblatt, *Principles of Neurodynamics: Perceptrons and the Theory of Brain Mechanisms* (Spartan Books, 1962), v.

17 For the definitive account of the development of American computing during the Cold War, see Paul N. Edwards, *The Closed World: Computers and the Politics of Discourse in Cold War America* (MIT Press, 1997).

involved in bringing new technologies into being. The histories that made these new insights possible are also rendered invisible through a focus on novelty. Thinking in terms of familial structures and the ways in which Rosenblatt might have thought of his own role as an academic, researcher, mentor, and friend might provide a useful frame of reference for understanding his work and his inventions. When Senator McCarthy called Rosenblatt a "universal brother," he was gesturing toward Rosenblatt's well-known care of others. Never knowing his own father, Rosenblatt turned himself into a role model and mentor to many. Given his inquiry into parenting practices in his early research, his lifelong interest in the transfer of learning, and most crucially his role within his community of friends, students, and collaborators, it would not be wrong to think of Rosenblatt as a father to many as well as a brother.

As his colleagues noted in his Cornell University obituary, the big problems that attracted Rosenblatt were not just scientific—they also included those experienced by human beings and especially those coming of age during the turbulent 1960s. With "a deep interest in student affairs and a personal concern which led him to help very many who had difficulties in adjusting to University life," Rosenblatt gathered together a diverse group of young people around him.[18] He provided support, shelter, counsel, and friendship to numerous Cornell students and others. The gathered "kids," as one former resident of his notorious farmhouse collective writes, included "Frank's graduate students; old friends; young men who were or had been his lovers; partners, siblings, partners of siblings, and siblings of partners of siblings of the above categories; sometimes boys who'd run away from reform school farther upstate."[19]

18 Stephen T. Emlen, Howard C. Howland, and Richard D. O'Brien, "Frank Rosenblatt," in *Memorial Statements of the Cornell University Faculty (1868–2009)*, ed. J. Robert Cooke, *Cornell eCommons*, 2010, https://hdl.handle.net/1813/19318.

19 Eve Kosofsky Sedgwick, quoted in Michael Moon et al., "Queers in (Single-Family) Space," *Assemblage* 24 (1994): 32–33.

Fig. 2.1. "Frank Rosenblatt." RMC2005_0770, Rare Book and Manuscript Collections, #41-2-877. Courtesy of the Division of Rare and Manuscript Collections, Cornell University Library.

An intensely private person who welcomed strangers into his home, Frank Rosenblatt was a contradictory figure. He was queer and was described by acquittances as having bisexual relationships with several people, including students or former students. He conducted research that was directly used by the US military and the CIA.[20] He was also an anti-war activist and ardent supporter of Eugene McCarthy. The details of his life and background remained mainly private, even to those who were

20 The CIA was especially interested in applying the Perceptron to its surveillance and reconnaissance activities. See Julia A. Irwin, "Artificial Worlds and Perceptronic Objects: The CIA's Mid-Century Automatic Target Recognition," *Grey Room* 97 (2024): 6–35.

closest to him. For many, the 1960s were a freeing and liberatory moment yet this was also a time of great suspicion and fear, especially for those with sexualities viewed as non-normative and who were connected to radical political positions and histories.

The Rosenblatt Family and Early Education

Frank Rosenblatt was born on July 11, 1928. His mother, Katherine C. (Golding) Rosenblatt raised him, first in New Rochelle, a suburb of New York City, and then in the Bronx. Katherine was born in Russia in 1885 and immigrated to the United States. During early childhood, Frank Rosenblatt's family lived at 102 Colonial Place, a quiet suburban street, in a two-and-a-half-story home that was built in 1924 and sold to its first owners, the Rosenblatt family. Frank would never know his father: Frank Ferdinand Rosenblatt died on November 6, 1927, approximately eight months before his youngest child, his namesake, was born. Frank Ferdinand's birthdate is commonly listed as May 11, 1884 (some records claim that he was born in 1882) and he is recorded as being born in the village of Luboml in Volhynia, Russia, presently part of Ukraine. He was born with the name Ephraim but went by Frank, at least after he arrived in the United States. His early education was religious, studying Hebrew and the Talmud in a yeshiva, as well as secular, in a Russian gymnasium. While in Russia, Frank Ferdinand became involved in an organization called the General Jewish Labour Bund of Lithuania, Poland, and Russia, known more simply as "the Bund." This early experience with labor organizing and Marxist politics would come to shape his academic interests and much of his life's work. He may have been arrested or merely was concerned about being arrested; either way, he permanently left his home and family at a young age.

Frank Ferdinand arrived in the United States in 1903, following his initial emigration from Russia to Switzerland. Shortly after he arrived in New York City, he began attending Columbia University as an undergraduate, during which time he studied economics, sociology, and philosophy. He earned his AB degree in 1907. With the support of a scholarship as a University Scholar, he stayed on at Columbia as a graduate student, earning his AM in 1908 for a thesis titled "M. Tugan Baranowsky and Other Russian Economists." On December 27, 1910 he married Katherine "Kitty" Golding in New York and they had two children in the next five years. From 1914 until 1916 he also served as the General Secretary of the Workmen's Circle, also known as the Arbeter Ring, which was then functioning as a major Jewish mutual aid organization.

Frank Ferdinand continued his research at Columbia while working for the Workmen's Circle and in 1917, he was awarded a PhD in Political Science for a dissertation titled "The Chartist Movement: In its Social and Economic Aspects." This dissertation, which was dedicated to Katherine "in appreciation of true comradeship," was published as a book and for many decades remained an important scholarly reference on this pivotal moment in British political history. It remains in print.[21] Following his graduate work, Frank Ferdinand went to work for the National Monetary Commission and the Tariff Board.

While historical and social analysis was what drove Frank Ferdinand's scholarly interests and career, he was also called to the arts, especially to literature and literary criticism. In 1925, he purchased the assets of Nicholas L. Brown, a failed publishing company, and renamed the company Frank-Maurice Inc. The name suggested the hope that Maurice, his ten-year-old son, would eventually join him in the enterprise. Frank-Maurice had an office at 15 West 37th Street in Manhattan and published a range of books, including several literary translations from French, Danish, and Greek, a handbook for journalists writing for newspapers, a biography of Abraham Lincoln for young readers, and a collection of Jewish tales and legends. While his dissertation was his only published book in English under his own name, Frank Ferdinand wrote many articles and may have also published poetry in Yiddish.

21 Frank F. Rosenblatt, *The Chartist Movement: In Its Social and Economic Aspects* (1916) (Routledge, 2020).

Once in the United States, Frank Ferdinand became a committed socialist and proponent of mutual aid organizations, especially for recent Jewish immigrants in the United States. He would spend the majority of his life working for two major Jewish non-profit organizations: the Joint Distribution Committee (JDC) and the Bureau of Jewish Social Research. His work on behalf of these organizations brought him back to Russia and other eastern European countries, including Lithuania and the newly established Czechoslovakia. He left New York on July 3, 1920 for Paris, then Copenhagen, and then Ukraine. He worked from Europe for several years; the Rosenblatt family's return to the United States was delayed in part by an unspecified illness experienced by the young Maurice. Nonetheless, Maurice would later describe his early youth spent mostly abroad as enjoyable and comfortable.

Navigating complex relations among the Soviets, Americans, and several European governments, Frank Ferdinand assisted in distributing funds raised from Americans and brought news back to the US on the numerous tragedies and deteriorating conditions in eastern Europe. Frank Ferdinand Rosenblatt was a major figure in these organizations and within early twentieth-century American Jewish life.[22] He died of unknown causes at his home on Saturday, November 6, 1927. In his conclusion to Frank Ferdinand Rosenblatt's extended obituary published in *The Jewish Social Service Quarterly*, Samuel A. Goldsmith wrote:

> He was a brave and honest man. Perhaps his task had been completed, perhaps his period of storm and stress could be closed only by the tragic accident that brought him peace. Wherever in the Jewish world there will be a need for a man of intellect, of courage, and of firmly-rooted honesty in crises

22 Michael Beizer, "Restoring Courage to Jewish Hearts: Frank Rosenblatt's Mission in Siberia in 1919," *East European Jewish Affairs* 39, no. 1 (2009): 35–56.

> that may come within that Jewish world, the name of Rosenblatt should and will inevitably spring to men's lips.[23]

Reports of his death were circulated widely as he was memorialized in newspapers and by many Jewish organizations. He was buried in the Workmen's Circle section of the Mount Carmel Cemetery in Queens, New York.

Frank Rosenblatt was the youngest of the three Rosenblatt children. He had two older siblings, the previously mentioned Maurice, born in 1915, and a sister named Bernice, born in 1912. Both Rosenblatt children were quite young when they lived in eastern Europe with their parents. Maurice attended private schools while his father worked to facilitate emigration and to provide financial support to the hundreds of thousands of Jewish people facing the violence and displacement of Russian pogroms. Despite the trauma experienced by their parents, Maurice described his upbringing as rather privileged: "I had the advantage of gifted parents, a European immersion, an accelerated childhood, and audacious self-confidence. That was my patrimony….My parents were children of the Enlightenment, mother a musician. We never owned a car, but we always had a grand piano. The leitmotiv as we were growing up was Chopin's preludes."[24] Just a few years after his father's death, Maurice went to the University of Wisconsin in Madison, graduating in 1936. He returned to the Bronx to live with his mother and brother, working as a secretary and founder of the New York City Coordinating Committee for Democratic Action.[25] Following the attack on Pearl Harbor and the entrance of the United States into World War II, Maurice joined the US Army as a criminal investigator and was assigned to New Guinea. After the war,

23 Samuel A. Goldsmith, "Dr. Frank F. Rosenblatt," *The Jewish Social Service Quarterly* 4, no. 2 (1927): 119.

24 Maurice Rosenblatt, quoted in Scates, *Maurice Rosenblatt and the Fall of Joseph McCarthy*, 51.

25 1940 US Census data (National Archives, https://www.archives.gov/research/census/1940) and Scates, *Maurice Rosenblatt and the Fall of Joseph McCarthy*, 55.

Maurice returned to the United States and in short time became a very well-connected and powerful lobbyist in Washington, DC.

Maurice Rosenblatt is perhaps best known for his work on behalf of the National Committee for an Effective Congress (NCEC), a bi-partisan political action committee that he co-founded with Eleanor Roosevelt, the wife of former US president Franklin D. Roosevelt, in 1948. It was the NCEC that coordinated the efforts that led to the eventual censure of Joseph McCarthy, a Republican US Senator from Wisconsin. Beginning in the early 1950s, McCarthy turned his attention toward what he saw as the dangerous influence of communists within the US. The Cold War culture of political hysteria and paranoia enabled McCarthy to make numerous accusations, even as others suspected his motives and claims from the beginning.

McCarthy was appointed chair of the Senate Committee on Government Operations in 1953 and with Roy Cohn, who McCarthy had made chief council of the "Truman Committee," or the Senate Permanent Subcommittee on Investigations, used their acquired power to investigate almost anyone they wished. Through the Truman Committee, McCarthy investigated numerous individuals in government offices, the US Army, and those working for defense contractors. Cohn and McCarthy began making numerous accusations and threats and made homosexuals and those McCarthy believed to be homosexuals a special target.

In his work for the NCEC, and through the creation of what he called the "McCarthy Clearing House," Maurice Rosenblatt secured support from many individuals in government and even sought the Pope's support in condemning McCarthy, as McCarthy was a Catholic. While Maurice Rosenblatt defended his opposition to McCarthy in ideological rather than personal terms, it would be hard not to understand his experiences as the son of an immigrant Jewish socialist, and as a civil rights and left-wing labor organizer himself, as undergirding his desire to take on McCarthy and his enablers.

Unlike his sister and brother who spent several years of their childhood in Europe, Frank Rosenblatt was born and raised in the United States. He was born in the house at 102 Colonial Place in New Rochelle and by the time of the 1940 US Census, was living in a rented apartment on Greystone Avenue in the Riverdale neighborhood of the Bronx with his mother and brother. Thirteen years older than Frank, Maurice had graduated from college and was stationed in New Guinea during much of Frank's formative years. Rosenblatt attended the Bronx High School of Science, a prestigious and newly created New York City public magnet school for students with a passionate interest in the study of math and science. Bronx Science, as the school is commonly known, was founded in 1938. It was all-male during Rosenblatt's time at the school and would become co-educational shortly after he graduated.

Rosenblatt left Bronx Science and New York City for Cornell University, in Ithaca, New York in 1946. He came to Cornell with the support of a scholarship from the State of New York and would remain affiliated with this institution in one way or another until his death. While Cornell did not provide support for every project and interest of Rosenblatt's, this intellectual community supplied him with mentors, collaborators, students, and funding for his entire career. Rosenblatt graduated from Cornell with his AB degree in 1950 with a major in social psychology. In his entry in the *Cornellian* yearbook of 1950, he lists his campus activities as including the German Club, Model UN, and the Civil Liberties Committee. Like his father and brother, Frank appeared interested and invested in political and social questions. He was a liberal from his undergraduate days and would become more involved in leftist politics during the late 1960s, even as these politics started to run against the priorities of the major funding agencies that supported his costly research.

Graduate Research at Cornell University

Rosenblatt conducted his graduate research under the supervision of a committee comprised of three members of the psychology department: William Wilson Lambert, Julian Hochberg, and Robert Brodie MacLeod. Lambert was a highly interdisciplinary academic researcher who came to Cornell in 1951 from Harvard University. At Cornell, Lambert held simultaneous appointments in three different departments: Anthropology, Psychology, and Sociology.[26] The intersection of these three social scientific departments made Lambert an ideal mentor for Frank Rosenblatt who, as early as his dissertation project, was already crossing several distinct fields of research.

The other members of Rosenblatt's committee brought expertise in perception and the biological basis of human vision. Robert MacLeod was a Gestalt psychologist. This branch of psychology is concerned with understanding the functioning of psychological systems rather than discrete components and was especially interested in understanding visual perception. MacLeod came to Cornell in 1948 from McGill University in Montreal, Canada to serve as chair of the university's psychology department, a role he held until 1953.[27] Julian Hochberg was the most junior member of Rosenblatt's dissertation committee. He was also a specialist in the human visual system. Like MacLeod, Hochberg was interested in framing his research through Gestalt theory. He was primarily interested in the neurobiological basis of perception, an approach that would come to form the core of Rosenblatt's understanding of the Perceptron. It is important to recognize that none of these psychologists were trained in computation or considered specialists in statistical methods. Rosenblatt's knowledge and expertise in computing and statistical methods was acquired alongside his studies in psychology as a necessary component of the analytical methods that he used in his early investigations in human behavior.

26 Donald P. Hayes, Robin M. Williams, and Bruce P. Halpern, "William W. Lambert," in *Memorial Statements of the Cornell University Faculty (1868–2009)*, ed. J. Robert Cooke, *Cornell eCommons*, 2005, https://ecommons.cornell.edu/bitstream/handle/1813/18349/Lambert_William_W_2005.pdf.

27 Urie Bronfenbrenner, Thomas A. Ryan, and James J. Gibson, "Robert Brodie MacLeod," in *Memorial Statements of the Cornell University Faculty (1868–2009)*, ed. J. Robert Cooke, *Cornell eCommons*, 1972, https://ecommons.cornell.edu/bitstream/handle/1813/18676/MacLeod_Robert_Brodie_1972.pdf.

As a graduate student, Rosenblatt developed statistical methods for the analysis of traditional survey-based behavioral studies. He also conducted his own studies to generate data for his new methods. These studies were comprised of a series of questions printed on a form with bubbles for the respondents to fill in with pencil to mark their answers. Such surveys were the dominant method of conducting psychological research during the 1950s. Rosenblatt, like others both then and now, administered his surveys to undergraduate students in his university. The answers, when tabulated and analyzed, provided Rosenblatt with an opportunity to learn more about these students, their family backgrounds, and their personality traits.

Rosenblatt's graduate research was marked by the influence of the theories and methods of the early 1950s. The scientific project at the core of Rosenblatt's doctoral research was typical of psychological research conducted during this time. While he was primarily interested in the brain rather than the mind — which is to say, empirical studies of the neural basis for cognition and human behavior — his graduate research project was behavioral in nature, although he did not initially make use of any animal data or other biological samples. Behaviorism, an approach to psychological research best exemplified by the work of B.F. Skinner, was then in vogue and studies using this methodology took as their main object of analysis the self-reporting of human subjects. Skinner advocated for a "special discipline," one that practiced what he called "the experimental analysis of behavior," and he conducted empirical studies on the relation between the individuals and their environments. "The behavior of individual organisms," he writes, "is studied in carefully controlled environments, and the relation between behavior and environment then formulated."[28] For Rosenblatt and his mentors and peers, the controlled environment, in the case of human subjects, might take the form of a laboratory-based session in which one responds to a survey. For animal-based experiments, the controlled environment would be an artificial-

28 B.F. Skinner, *About Behaviorism* (Knopf Doubleday, 1976), 8.

ly constructed experimental apparatus with levers or buttons. These levers might dispense food or activate an environmental interaction with the animal, such as displaying a light, playing a noise, or even "punishing" the animal with a shock. This apparatus is frequently termed a Skinner box. It enabled, through its artificial construction, the reproducible study of responses to stimuli as well as the conditioning, which is to say, the modification of behavior in relation to the environment and stimuli.

The reinforcement of behaviors in response to reward and punishment was called operant conditioning. This paradigm of punishment and reward structured Rosenblatt's approach to machine learning and remains embedded, residually, in the reinforcement learning from human feedback (RLHF) mechanisms used to fine-tune contemporary Large Language Models (LLMs). This early science of reinforcement learning, which would become very important to the discourse of machine learning, preceded the cognitive science revolution that informs present-day psychological research. To create a new understanding of brain function, the new cognitive sciences would draw heavily on Rosenblatt's research, particularly his groundbreaking biological insights produced by his mechanical models.

Like much of his other scientific work, Rosenblatt's Cornell University doctoral dissertation, "The *k*-coefficient: Design and Trial Application of a New Technique for Multivariate Analysis," had an almost equal commitment to a deep interest in human behavior and the development of novel computational techniques. He defended this dissertation in February of 1956. In the dissertation, Rosenblatt provides a detailed summary and analysis of a small survey-based study of Cornell students on the "relationship of family background to students' future plans," and more importantly for his future career, the design and function of a specialized computer that he used to process the survey responses.[29] His dissertation also provided him with

29 Frank Rosenblatt, "The *k*-Coefficient: Design and Trial Application of a New Technique for Multivariate Analysis" (PhD diss., Cornell University, 1956), 79.

an opportunity to look back on the development of statistical and analytical methods and procedures that would guide much of his future research. The development of computer systems, the engineering of hardware and devices, and the creation of new or reformulated computational methods were always of equal interest to Rosenblatt as the more applied scientific goals of his research. Rosenblatt's extremely active scientific research program and many novel inventions and solutions were often effaced by his modest self-presentation and extreme humility. Later, shortly before his untimely death, he would defend his engineering and computational work by saying that he was a mere discoverer of certain methods and techniques. He believed that his approaches, in his work with constructing mechanical learning machines and simulations of them in software, were only synthetic instances of already existing biological operations.

While conducting the behavioral research that would be used in his dissertation, Rosenblatt made use of several different computer systems that were available to him. He used computational resources proved by the Cornell Computing Center (CCC), located on the university campus in Ithaca as well as the systems at the Cornell Aeronautical Laboratory (CAL) in Buffalo. Perhaps most importantly, he developed his own computing hardware. Rosenblatt called his device the Electronic Profile Analyzing Computer, or EPAC. He outlines the purpose, construction, and operation of the EPAC in Appendix G, "Design of the EPAC," of his dissertation and this system will be described further below in relation to his research trajectory and the invention of his mechanical learning machines. Rosenblatt's thoughtfully constructed appendix on the design for a specialized computer anticipates his work on such systems, including the Perceptron and its two major hardware implementations.

While the dissertation's primary focus is the introduction and analysis of his newly invented statistical method, the *k*-coefficient, Rosenblatt needed to run a traditional, behavioral psychological study to create and demonstrate his statistical method. The *k*-coefficient, in Rosenblatt's words, "is a technique for estimating multiple correlations for much larger numbers of variables than can be handled by conventional statistics."[30] Contemporary statistical methods use multiple regression and least squares to find coefficients. Coefficients, in the case of the psychological research conducted in this period, would be variables representing various aspects of behavioral traits. These "aspects" would, hopefully, have correlated relations with multiple different survey responses. He proposed the *k*-coefficient as an alternative to the standard statistical methods used to analyze these data. It would estimate coefficients by comparing pairs of already-processed data and calculating, from the resulting matrix of pair-wise comparisons, a curve in which the lowest point would be the *k* value for that group of variables. Beyond the ability to handle many variables, the chief value of the *k*-coefficient is that it enables a researcher to "measure the net effects of a collection of independent variables upon a group of dependent variables simultaneously, rather than computing a separate correlation for each dependent variable."[31] Rosenblatt notes in the introduction to his dissertation that the behavioral surveys used in research were becoming much more complex and the calculations required were beginning to overwhelm contemporary general-purpose digital computers:

> In computing a multiple correlation coefficient (or solving a multiple regression equation) the amount of computation involved goes up roughly with the cube of the number of variables. Thus if 1000 steps are needed for a multiple correlation of five variables, then 8000 steps would be needed for 10 variables, 27,000 steps for 15 variables, and 64,000 steps for 20 variables. This progression will rapidly exceed the limits of even the fastest digital computers.[32]

In order to develop this new statistical method for calculating coefficients in a more computationally efficient manner, Rosen-

30 Ibid., 1.
31 Ibid., 24.
32 Ibid., 2.

blatt would have needed to have borrowed another researcher's dataset of sufficient complexity or developed his own survey instrument. He decided to design his own. This would require collecting a large amount of self-reported survey-based data. As previously mentioned, these were behavioral surveys or questionnaires — they are termed behavioral because the research paradigm was based on observation and the reported activity of individuals in the world rather than groups of people within artificial environments. The questions would address different aspects of behavior that would be mapped or correlated with multiple variables or coefficients. Already one can recognize Rosenblatt's strong investment in researching computationally intensive applications that exceed the capacity of digital computers.

Rosenblatt framed his small experiment as personality research. It was not empirically validated, as he writes in the dissertation, because he did not have an outside observer collect data on the independent variables and he depended upon the subjects to use their own judgment in recalling past experiences and answering questions. Nonetheless, this study's real purpose was to test and analyze his new statistical procedure and this survey data would be adequate to assess the methods. Rosenblatt describes his modest behavioral experiment as "a study of the relationships of early family experience to adult anxiety and personality patterns."[33] The questionnaires would be used to create personality "profiles" from responses to multiple choice questions and Likert-scaled responses. The Likert scale, commonly used in social-scientific research and in consumer or educational assessments, asks respondents to check or otherwise select a response from a five-point scale. These scales typically range from 1 (Strongly Agree) to 5 (Strongly Disagree). Rosenblatt also used a variant in which he presented two different statements in the same question. The survey instructions, reproduced in his dissertation, were as follows:

33 Ibid., 34.

> In most of the items in these questionnaires, you will find two contrasting statements, with a five-point scale between them, as follows:
>
> Statement A Statement B
>
> (1) (2) (3) (4) (5)
>
> You are to check one point on the scale, to indicate how closely you agree with statement A or B. If you agree closely with Statement A, then you would check Point 1. If you agree closely with Statement B, then you would check Point 5. You should check only one point on each scale.[34]

Rosenblatt would then construct profiles from his statistical analysis of the possible correlations found among his collected responses.

Rosenblatt's dissertation research was conducted under the frame of the "Pattern Correlation Project." The survey data and Rosenblatt's conception of learning itself is saturated with the logics of behaviorism, which, as mentioned above, was the dominant form of social psychology during the period. Many of his survey questions addressing "early family experience" were aimed at understanding parenting roles and responsibilities as well as asking subjects to recall their experiences during the first twelve years of life. In focusing on parental roles and upbringing, the survey implicitly understood adult behavior as linked to childhood experiences. Rosenblatt was especially interested in how anxiety was correlated with parenting practices—which is to say, reinforced learning from experience. Some of the questions he used for this survey included:

> 8-9. During my first twelve years, my mother was always very critical of things that I did or planned; she always

34 Ibid., 82.

Fig. 2.2. Frank Rosenblatt and Eugene "Gene" Endres. Courtesy of William Mutch.

seemed to find something wrong no matter what I was doing.
She practically never criticized me during this period; she hated to express criticism under any circumstances.
[...]

11-27. My father was always scolding about something, and would give me a severe tongue-lashing if I did something wrong.
He hardly ever mentioned anything that I did wrong, and would never scold me, in any case.[35]

35 Ibid., 90–91, 110–11.

The survey questions were organized around the figures being recalled and assessed. The subject's mother, father, and siblings formed the basic family group, while another section addressed the subject's relations to their childhood friends, separated by gender.

Rosenblatt initially contacted a random sampling of 300 undergraduate students at Cornell. He was able to collect survey responses from 201 of these 300 students (he had responses from 133 male students and 68 female students).[36] They were paid $3.00 for their time and a control group of students were asked to complete the survey as part of their coursework in psychology. Self-reported data was collected from the student subjects, automatically read and scored from paper forms and rating sheets using graphite pencils, and eventually stored in processed form on two sets of IBM punch cards, one set representing the raw data and the other set of cards containing corrected data, which accounted for any missing data.

Rosenblatt designed the EPAC, a truly single-purpose computer, to read pairs of paper survey forms, not industry-standard IBM punch cards. The EPAC took the form of what would now be considered a pre-processor. It read raw data from the forms answered by his research subjects and outputted standardized data along with some basic statistical processing that would make later processing and interpretation on traditional computer systems easier. It did not calculate the *k*-coefficient but rather what were called D^2 values. These were the intermediate values, produced from the survey responses, that were used to produce the pair-wise matrix of coefficients, which were the experimental variables attached to predicted aspects of human behavior. Rosenblatt conducted further processing of his data, including generating the *k*-coefficients and higher-level statistics, on general purpose computers at Cornell and CAL.

During Rosenblatt's time, Cornell's psychology department was housed in Justin Morrill Hall and it was there that Rosenb-

36 Rosenblatt, "Appendix D: Questionnaire Item Distributions," in "The *k*-Coefficient," 169–84.

Fig. 2.3. Frank Rosenblatt with EPAC system in Morrill Hall. *Cornell Alumni Magazine,* December 1, 1953. Courtesy of William Mutch.

latt constructed and used the EPAC computer. Morrill Hall was named after Vermont Senator Justin Smith Morrill who had advocated for what became known as the Morrill Land-Grant Colleges Act of 1862. Within Morrill Hall, Rosenblatt put together what he would come to call the "idiot brain" of the EPAC computer. What made the EPAC an "idiot brain" was that the device was not capable of executing a large number of instructions; in fact, its only purpose was to calculate *k*-coefficients by comparing behavioral profiles. It was also an "idiot brain" because it was just the germ of the model that Rosenblatt dreamed of building, the smallest building block of his desired brain model. Rosenblatt's brain model would be a more complex device that simulated a network of neurons; the EPAC merely executed a single transformation: the calculation of a set of values from supplied input using a hardware-encoded algorithm. Nonetheless, in both its informal name and in its construction, the EPAC represented a significant step forward in constructing mechanical devices that would eventually model neurons and become the building block of neural networks.

Captivated by the notion that computers could be built that would resemble the brain and that perhaps the brain itself was a computer, Rosenblatt's larger and deferred goal was to construct a machine that could think and reason and interpret the world—a thinking machine. The EPAC could not learn and could not even recognize patterns. It was only capable of mechanically producing comparisons of data read from pairs of forms and generating output that he would later analyze on more powerful computers. Despite the simplicity of the EPAC it was an achievement and marked Rosenblatt as distinct within his field; among his peers doing high-level graduate research at the forefront of scientific discovery, especially within a psychology department, it was incredibly rare for someone to design and build any sort of computing system.

Rosenblatt did not start from scratch in designing the EPAC; he modeled some of the major components of the EPAC on what is now one of the best-known earliest computers, the ENIAC, or Electronic Numerical Integrator and Computer. These components were used to store data and required a significant amount of engineering; his borrowing of this design enabled him to focus on implementing just the hardware components needed to perform the calculations on the stored values. The ENIAC was created in 1945 with funding from the US Army Ordnance Corps and it was housed on the campus of the University of Pennsylvania, in Philadelphia. It served as inspiration for many of the computer designs that would follow.[37]

Engineering Research Associates had described in detail the construction and operation of this system which was also described in a textbook titled *High Speed Computing Devices* (1950). Rosenblatt used these insights from the operation of ENIAC to build his own special-purpose computer and the experience would be crucial for imagining an alternative design for

37 Thomas Haigh, Mark Priestly, and Crispin Rope, *ENIAC in Action: Making and Remaking the Modern Computer* (MIT Press, 2016).

a computing machine that could be said to learn not through traditional programming but through seeing a series of samples, a process not unlike the scanning of form data performed by the EPAC. While the EPAC was a very small-scale computer that was "programmed" for only a single operation, for Rosenblatt, this hand-built computer was extremely important. It was important not only because it was an answer to a limitation found in general purpose digital computers but also because it enabled him to engineer a device that would give him dedicated access to computing hardware. At that time, digital computers were expensive, rare, and shared. By offloading some of his calculations from a digital computer, Rosenblatt had what was essentially a desktop computing device that he could use whenever he wanted and for as long as he wanted.

Rosenblatt's very first academic publication appeared the year of his dissertation defense. With two other researchers at Cornell, James J. Gibson, a psychologist, and Paul Olum, a mathematician, Rosenblatt co-authored an article titled "Parallax and Perspective During Aircraft Landings."[38] Like almost all of Rosenblatt's later research, this project was supported by funding from the United States military, in this case, the United States Air Force. Curiously, the article begins by adapting a concept, the parallax, from astronomy, the field addressed by Rosenblatt's final, posthumously published research essay. Gibson had served in the Air Force during World War II, conducting military research, and he continued some of this work at Cornell. "Parallax and Perspective During Aircraft Landings" concerned the creation of a mathematical model of motion perspective, a key problem for understanding the configuration of the visual field as a pilot approaches the ground from the air.

According to a graduate student who later worked with both Gibson and Rosenblatt, Rosenblatt came upon Gibson and Olum working on the mathematical model on a blackboard and

38 James J. Gibson, Paul Olum, and Frank Rosenblatt, "Parallax and Perspective During Aircraft Landings," *The American Journal of Psychology* 68, no. 3 (1955): 372–85.

assisted them in their work, thus earning co-authorship. This early publication would come to inform some of Rosenblatt's early imagined problems for the Perceptron — the categorization of visual data, especially those from aerial reconnaissance photography, were the original problems the Perceptron was funded to solve — and he would continue to interact with Gibson and especially with his wife, Eleanor Gibson, a psychologist interested in the perceptual development of infants. In their cultural analysis of the concept of affordance in media history, Erica Robles-Anderson and Scott Ferguson have shown that Eleanor Gibson was a key figure in the development of affordance theory, which has been important to many fields.[39] They show the influence of her experimental work on what is called the visual cliff, the impression of a dramatic drop through the manipulation of depth cues, on design theory and the development of early computer vision. In the early 1960s, Rosenblatt would replicate Eleanor Gibson's experiments teaching pre-literate infants to discriminate between similar alphabetical characters to produce training models for the Perceptron. In more than one instance Rosenblatt compared the training of the Perceptron to the training and education of children and in adapting Gibson's experimental design and stimuli for machine learning, he was interested in the possibility that learning and perception functioned in similar ways for his neural networks and for children.[40]

It was during this same time, while still a graduate student, that Rosenblatt started work as an engineer at Cornell Aeronautical Laboratory. CAL, as the lab was called, was in Buffalo, New York, about one-hundred-and-fifty miles from Cornell's campus in Ithaca. Formerly owned by the Curtiss-Wright Aircraft Corporation, the lab conducted aeronautical research and built aircraft for the US military during World War II. Cornell University

39 Erica Robles-Anderson and Scott Ferguson, "The Visual Cliff: Eleanor Gibson & the Origins of Affordance," *Money on the Left*, April 19, 2022, https://moneyontheleft.org/2022/04/19/the-visual-cliff-eleanor-gibson-the-origins-of-affordance/.

40 James E. Dobson, "On the Confusion Matrix," *Configurations* 32, no. 4 (2024): 331–50.

took over the operation of the facility in 1946, shortly after the end of the war. While Rosenblatt had started his research into machine learning on the Cornell campus in Ithaca, CAL would become the origin site of the Perceptron and Rosenblatt's collaborators and colleagues would continue his applied research into machine learning using his invention after he left.

Research conducted at CAL was primarily supported by the US military (mainly through contracts awarded by the US Air Force and US Navy) and the Perceptron was no exception. The Information Systems Branch of the Office of Navy Research (ONR) had funded Rosenblatt's Perceptron research beginning in July of 1957. Rosenblatt's research was supported through two funding mechanisms, a contract awarded to CAL (Nor 2381-00) and one awarded to Cornell University (Nor 401-40). Once leaving CAL for Cornell, Rosenblatt would continue to be funded under Nor 401-40 until 1971. The first publication addressing the Perceptron was a research report that made the case for additional funding for the project. Almost all subsequent reports and peer-reviewed publications acknowledged the funding of the ONR. This source of funding did not appear to initially bother Rosenblatt; he worked closely with ONR officials and referenced military applications in the initial and other proposals for the project. Cornell Aeronautical Laboratory, in the decade after World War II, positioned itself as a resource for Cold War technoscience, especially projects linked to visual surveillance and air superiority. In the early 1970s, in response to student protests directed toward Cornell's involvement in research that was being deployed in the Vietnam War, the university divested itself of the laboratory by creating the Calspan Corporation to manage the facility.

Developing the Neural Net Model for Learning

In 1943, Warren S. McCulloch and his student Walter Pitts published a ground-breaking paper, "A Logical Calculus of Ideas

Immanent in Nervous Activity."[41] This paper developed a formal description of the operation of a neuron and introduced this model to a number of scientific communities. The "McCulloch-Pitts" model provided the mathematical conceptualization of a simplified set of neurons that inspired more than a few scientists to explore the potential for new ways of processing data and information enabled by this model. The McCulloch-Pitts model imagined the nervous system as composed of a "net of neurons" and described in simplified terms the process of neuronal excitation by which impulses might move through such a net. This mathematical model influenced many mid-twentieth-century researchers working at the intersection of psychology and engineering as it provided a formal and electronic account of biological systems involved in information processing.

In 1949, the psychologist Donald O. Hebb revised this model of neural activity to include propositions about the relation between these observed and modeled patterns of neural activity and learning. *The Organization of Behavior: A Neuropsychological Theory,* Hebb's book-length account of learning and perception in humans and animals, would give Rosenblatt the major inspiration for his neural network design for recognizing and storing patterns of information. At the time of the book's publication, Hebb had recently arrived at McGill University from the Florida-based Yerkes Laboratories of Primate Biology in Florida. Hebb had occupied the chair of the psychology department that was vacated when Rosenblatt's advisor Robert MacLeod came to Cornell University. Hebb's account of perception made some departure from the Gestalt theories studied and developed by MacLeod and others in Rosenblatt's department.[42] In particular,

41 Warren S. McCulloch and Walter S. Pitts, "A Logical Calculus of the Ideas Immanent in Nervous Activity," *Bulletin of Mathematical Biophysics* 5 (1943): 115. On what has been termed the "homosocial" milieu of this research relationship, see Elizabeth A. Wilson, *Affect and Artificial Intelligence* (University of Washington Press, 2010), 126.

42 As Hebb explains this departure from Gestalt theory, "Attention is drawn to this aspect [the influence of experience on visual perception] of Gestalt theory because it helps one to define the point at which one can diverge

as Hebb argues, Gestalt theory proposes that in recognizing an object, "one perceives a simple figure (such as square or circle), one perceives it directly as a distinctive whole, without need of any learning process and not through a prior recognition of the several parts of the figure."[43] This was not how perception worked in Hebb's model. On the contrary, figures — which is to say, wholes — were learned through prior recognition of component parts.

Hebb's model was used by a research group at IBM, led by Nathaniel Rochester, who implemented a version of this neural model for learning by constructing what they called, after Hebb, "cell assemblies." According to Hebb, a cell assembly names a theoretical collection of neurons that are not formed by design — and in the case of simulated neurons, not created by programmers — but through practice, which is to say, through learning. These multiple assemblies would be developed over time, as neurons were activated or stimulated. An assembly might become specialized and correspond to a particular class of inputs; with visual input, an assembly might be formed by groups of neurons that were activated when seeing objects with similar shapes or features. As Rosenblatt explains, "Hebb proposes that a set of neurons which is repeatedly activated by a particular sensory stimulus becomes organized into a functional unit, which can be triggered as a whole by sensory patterns sufficiently similar to the original one."[44] Hoping that this theory could be implemented in simulated neurons in learning machines, and assemblies created to recognize letters or people or military aircraft, researchers sought to design networks that could become self-organized. In their paper, titled "Tests

---

from the theory without failing to recognize the great contribution it has made to modern psychology, which has been shaped to a great extent by the impact of Gestalt ideas on behaviorism." Donald O. Hebb, *The Organization of Behavior: A Neuropsychological Theory* (1949; repr. Taylor & Francis, 2002), 66.

43 Ibid., 17–18.

44 Frank Rosenblatt, "Perceptron Simulation Experiments," *Proceedings of the IRE* 48, no. 3 (1960): 301.

on a Cell Assembly Theory of the Action of the Brain, Using a Large Digital Computer," Rochester and his colleagues describe the complexities of implementing this theory in simulated neurons, in software, on their computers: "Hebb's theory required that it be possible for a neuron to belong to several different cell assemblies and that not all of these assemblies be aroused at once. Hebb's theory also required that it be possible for a neuron to change its affiliation from one cell assembly to another."[45] Rosenblatt cites the IBM work in his explication of his Perceptron model and introduces his innovation as a variation on this model. Rosenblatt described the IBM cell assembly model as resulting in "ambiguous" results and lacking definition vis a vis the object to be modeled. He also introduced some randomness into the connections that make up the network, a concept that will be explored further shortly.

Rosenblatt's main intellectual project with the Perceptron, as he outlined in one of his first academic articles on the concept, was to develop an answer to these three fundamental biological questions in a single computer system:

1. How is information about the physical world sensed, or detected, by the biological system?
2. In what form is information stored, or remembered?
3. How does information contained in storage, or in memory, influence recognition and behavior?[46]

A neural network that was directly connected to a sensing system, a system capable of reliably encoding input from the physical world, would provide some degree of a response to all three of Rosenblatt's research questions.

45 N. Rochester, J. Holland, L. Haibt, and W. Duda, "Tests on a Cell Assembly Theory of the Action of the Brain, Using a Large Digital Computer," *IEEE Transactions on Information Theory* 2, no. 3 (1956): 80–93.

46 Frank Rosenblatt, "The Perceptron: A Probabilistic Model for Information Storage and Organization in the Brain," *Psychological Review* 65, no. 6 (1958): 386–408.

The visual-perceptual system, and the retina, specifically, was his primary model for detecting and encoding sensed information about the world. In basing his neural network on the visual perceptron model, Rosenblatt created a simple "machine" that would take already existing knowledge about the world and encode it through quantization in a set of stored variables, values that he called weights, that registered information and could be adjusted and slowly altered. This process of adjustment was influenced by an operator or teacher who either directly or indirectly altered the weights by "reinforcing" or tilting them toward the correct answer until they eventually represented "correct" values as a response to input stimuli.

As Rosenblatt said in response to an audience question about the Perceptron project at a conference in 1960,

> Well, first of all let me say that we are interested in duplicating human learning, if it is possible to do so. We are interested in determining the extent to which it is feasible to consider such a thing as duplicating human learning, or at least understanding how human learning operates. Whether or not there exists a better mode of learning is in a sense an empirical question to which I don't feel we can supply an answer at this point.... We are interested, however, not only in studying human learning, but in studying the behavior of networks which include biological nervous systems as a subclass. This is to say, we are interested in the study of signal transmission networks which involve connected nodes or cell points which have functional characteristics similar to those of biological neurons, but not necessarily better.[47]

Rosenblatt's major interest was in modeling and replicating the ways in which our brains make us essentially what he thought

47 Frank Rosenblatt, "Perceptual Generalization Over Transformation Groups," in *Self-Organizing Systems: Proceedings of an Interdisciplinary Conference,* ed. Marshall C. Yovits and Scott Cameron (Pergamon Press, 1960), 97.

of as biological learning machines. In time, Rosenblatt would increasingly make it clear that his invention was primarily intended to be a brain model. It was not, he argued forcefully in the preface to his 1962 *Principles of Neurodynamics,* a specialized device for pattern recognition nor should it be considered a component of artificial intelligence. Rosenblatt's motivations for drawing this distinction were most likely defensive. There had been several published reports on the application of the Perceptron concept for pattern recognition, especially for military use, and the discourse on artificial intelligence, which was already almost a decade old, was attracting new attention from scientists and the general public, most of it quite critical. Rosenblatt notes this in the opening paragraphs of *Principles of Neurodynamics:* "the aims and methods of perceptron research are in need of clarification is apparent from the extent of the controversy within the scientific community since 1957, concerning the value of the perceptron concept."[48] He responds to the "negative reactions" to his research by attempting to reframe his project and disavow some of his earlier efforts to link his work to applied problems in computer vision and to his own preemptive attempts to publicize the Perceptron by engaging with reporters and conducting public demonstrations.

As his research questions indicate, Rosenblatt's early goal was to construct "a machine capable of learning closely analogous to the perceptual processes of a biological brain."[49] It would operate roughly according to the theory outlined by Hebb, that the visual perception of objects was "not immediately given but slowly acquired through learning" and that it depended upon a *"pattern of excitation* whose locus is unimportant."[50] Learning would thus involve the repeated presentation of stimuli that would be "stored" as economized memories of previously seen

48 Ibid., v.

49 Rosenblatt, "The Perceptron: A Perceiving and Recognizing Automaton," 2.

50 Ibid., 35, 17.

patterns. The history of acquired patterns would be stored in memory and this would enable later retrieval and correction.

As a solution to the problem of how to store and determine distinctions between randomly presented and previously seen samples (for example, squares and circles), Rosenblatt proposed a linear algorithm that he called the "theory of statistical separability," which has now become known as the perceptron convergence theorem. Given a selection of two classes of objects and a possible difference between the two classes as exhibited in the input data, such as pixel-like representations of the letters "E" and "F," the Perceptron would eventually "converge" upon a solution through the linear separation of the two samples.[51] Through this separation of data, the Perceptron is able to correctly classify new input as belonging to the correct class in this binary model, meaning either an "E" or "F." For this approach to work, the data have to be separable, which is to say that, in the examples of "E" and "F," there needs to be a clear difference. Here are reproductions of example representations used by Rosenblatt:

XXXXXXXXXXXX	XXXXXXXXXXXX
XXXXXXXXXXXX	XXXXXXXXXXXX
XX	XX
XX	XX
XX	XX
XX	XX
XXXXXXXXXXXX	XXXXXXXXXXXX
XXXXXXXXXXXX	XXXXXXXXXXXX
XX	XX
XX	XX
XX	XX
XX	XX
XXXXXXXXXXXX	XX
XXXXXXXXXXXX	XX

51 These were the letters and representations used in some early Perceptron experiments. See Carl Kesler and Frank Rosenblatt, "Further Simulation Experiments on Series-Coupled Perceptrons," in *Collected Technical Papers*, vol. 5, report no. 5: Cognitive Systems Research Program, ed. Frank Rosenblatt (Cornell University, 1963), 73–98.

The difficulty in finding separable data, which depends so much upon its representation (in the case of recognizing an "E" or "F," the features would be pixel-like values with a considerable amount of overlap), and the philosophical stakes of labeling something a "class" were key factors in the limited uptake of the original Perceptron neural network paradigm.

Despite these issues, the eventual convergence toward a solution, to finding the criteria that would produce the linear separation between two classes, worked and would eventually prove the validity of this idea. This core concept — eventually, a mathematically solid approach — would come to characterize the Perceptron so much that in their account of the history of artificial intelligence, Martin A. Fischler and Oscar Firschein, two foundational figures in computer vision and AI, indexed it as a "threshold device."[52] The threshold in this case is the rule or formula that determines classification based on what has been learned from the examples used as training data. Once trained, the model has learned the threshold values. Rosenblatt provided an example that highlights the role of the human operator in the reinforcement style of learning used by the Perceptron:

> It is possible to teach the system to discriminate two such generalized forms, or "percepts," by presenting for each form a random sample from the set of its possible transformations, while simultaneously "forcing" the system to respond with Output 1 for Form 1, and Output 2 for Form 2. For example, we might require the perceptron to learn the concepts "square" and "circle," and to turn on Signal Light 1 for "square," and Signal Light 2 for "circle." We would then proceed to show the system a large set of squares of different sizes, in different locations, while holding Light No. 1 on, thus "forcing" the response. We would then show a similar set of circles, while holding Light No. 2 on. If we then show the perceptron *any* square or *any* circle, we would expect it

52 Martin A. Fischler and Oscar Firschein, *Intelligence: The Eye, the Brain, and the Computer* (Addison-Wesley, 1987), 138–40.

> to turn on the appropriate light, with a high probability of being correct.[53]

Learning in this paradigm involved the use of operator-assisted feedback in the form of "forcing" the correct response. Present-day machine learning methods typically pair labels identifying the correct concept, category, or response with training data to provide this same sort of supervised training.

While influenced by the roughly contemporary neuroscientific accounts of brain function, Rosenblatt's early descriptions of his proposed reinforcement learning procedure, especially in his account of "teaching" the Perceptron to recognize patterns as forcing the correct response, also draws from some of the behavioralist assumptions found in his dissertation study on parenting practices. Take, for example, the previously invoked example survey question: "My father was always scolding about something, and would give me a severe tongue-lashing if I did something wrong."[54] Rosenblatt's conception of the training procedures from his system rendered the operator of the machine, by virtue of the data presented to the model, much like the father in this example. He describes this as such: "If the positive and negative reinforcement can be controlled by the application of external stimuli, they become essentially equivalent to 'reward' and 'punishment,' and can be used in this sense by the experimenter."[55] The forcing of a response and the environment itself, the external stimuli presented to the Perceptron, alter the behavior of the system in ways that are not unlike the concept of operant conditioning in mid-twentieth-century behaviorism.

The Perceptron was intended as a simulation of a nervous system; it was to be a "perceiving" machine that would sense environmental stimuli and respond by producing associations that would result in the identification or classification of the input

53 Rosenblatt, "The Perceptron: A Perceiving and Recognizing Automaton," 3.

54 Rosenblatt, "The *k*-Coefficient," 110–11.

55 Rosenblatt, "The Perceptron: A Probabilistic Model," 402.

stimulus. Contemporary digital computers operated on coded information and Rosenblatt proposed to his employers at the Cornell Aeronautical Laboratory that they create "a machine which would be capable of conceptualizing inputs impinging *directly from the physical environment* of light, sound, temperature, etc. — the 'phenomenal world' with which we are all familiar — rather than requiring the intervention of a human agent to digest and code the necessary information."[56] The dream of connecting computers directly to the environment was widely shared during the mid-twentieth century. This dream persisted despite the fact that the machinery required occupied large amounts of physical space. The mobility required to enable digital systems, as self-contained systems, to interact with their environment was several decades away. If the Perceptron was to directly sense the physical environment, it would need to have sophisticated mechanisms for acquiring sensory data.

The Perceptron was imagined as having a grid or mosaic of sensors that would operate like the retina of an eye — the mechanical sensing device was called a retina — with each sensor representing a point within the retinal space. This space was originally defined as a 20 x 20 mosaic of light-sensitive sensors. These could be photocells or another mechanism for acquiring image data. Patterns would be detected by the active points found within this space. While they could be moved to different locations, it was what we would now call a "low-resolution" device and the centers of stimuli would need to be located within a smaller 5 x 5-point window within the center of the "retina." These retinal points were the equivalent of the smallest elements that make up digitized visual data, elements that would later be called pixels. These points allowed for the sensing of the presence or absence of stimuli. The various patterns of "activated" points represented a digitized representation of the sensed two-dimensional objects. This model of vision, coupled with a camera and quantizing hardware, would enable the Perceptron to discriminate between two categories of simple visual objects.

---

56 Rosenblatt, "The Perceptron: A Perceiving and Recognizing Automaton," 1.

In order to store, transform, and make decisions based on these activated retinal points, the Perceptron would need a network of other modules. Rosenblatt proposed using three different sets of the previously mentioned simplified McCulloch-Pitts neurons to create his initial neural net. These sets of simplified neurons were known as the S, A, and R units. The S units made up the sensory system and were imagined as the 20 x 20-"point" retinal mosaic. The A units were association units, which summed the activation values from the S units, which would be connected to some number of different A units. The connections would be either positive, "excitatory" connections, or negative, "inhibitory" connections. The A units would in turn be connected to a smaller number of R or response units. These were activated by some number of A units reaching a pre-defined threshold value. By 1959 Rosenblatt was describing his invention as a "nerve net" and making explicit, by organizational analogy, the degree to which his system was intended to simulate actual existing biological structures:

> A simplified version of a mammalian visual system is shown in Figure 1, for a comparison with the organization of a perceptron, which will be described presently. At the extreme left we see a mosaic of light-sensitive points, or retina, from which signals are transmitted to the visual projection area, in the cerebral cortex. Several intermediate relay stations exist in a typical biological system, which are not shown here. These connections preserve topological characteristics of the stimulus in a reasonably intact form. Beyond the projection area, however, connections appear to be largely random. Impulses are delivered through a large number of paths to the association areas of the cortex, where local feedback loops are activated, so that activity may persist for some time past the termination of the original visual stimulus. From the association area, signals are transmitted to the motor cortex,

> which again has a clear topological organization corresponding to the location of muscle groups to be controlled.[57]

In the years following the invention of the Perceptron, Rosenblatt underwent a transformation in how he described the Perceptron, from presenting it, especially to funding agencies and the media, initially as a general-purpose pattern recognition device toward describing it as a synthetic brain. Framings of the Perceptron as a neural model were certainly common in the early years, as we see above, but the fallout from both the public reaction to the Perceptron and critiques launched at him from his colleagues, the above-mentioned reference by Rosenblatt to the "controversy within the scientific community," required Rosenblatt to reposition his invention.[58]

Announcing and Simulating the Perceptron

In his proposal to the Cornell Aeronautical Laboratory, dated April 3, 1957, for what was to become Project PARA, Rosenblatt describes the "electronic automaton" that he plans to build through an ambitious pilot project expected to take eighteen months:

> Establishment of a new research program at Cornell Aeronautical Laboratory, Inc. is proposed, with the objective of designing, fabricating, and evaluating an electronic brain model, the *photoperceptron*. The proposed pilot model will be capable of "learning" responses to ordinary visual patterns, or forms. The system will employ a new theory of memory storage (the theory of *statistical separability*), which permits

57 Frank Rosenblatt, "Perceptron Simulation Experiments (Project Para)," Report No. VG-1196-6-3, Cornell Aeronautical Laboratory, June 1959.

58 For more on these debates and controversies, which mostly concerned the presentation of mathematical proof of the Perceptron convergence theorem and formal descriptions of neural networks, see Mikel Olazaran, "A Sociological Study of the Official History of the Perceptrons Controversy," *Social Studies of Science* 26, no. 3 (1996): 611–59.

> the recognition of complex patterns with an efficiency far greater than that attainable by existing computers. Devices of this sort are expected ultimately to be capable of concept formation, language translation, collocation of military intelligence and the solution of problems through inductive logic.[59]

The proposal outlined the construction of a photoperceptron, the initial class of Perceptron devices imagined by Rosenblatt and the easiest to implement. The photoperceptron was a key component in the development of early computer vision techniques. It was imagined within the intersection of the logics of 1950s televisual culture and the contemporary understanding of the biological basis of perception. As the abstract concept of the Perceptron was modeled on biological visual systems, the machine Rosenblatt would eventually build used conventional television cameras and focused on visual perception. Until that machine was built, however, Rosenblatt would have to simulate the operation of a Perceptron on a conventional digital computer and make do, initially, with simplified encoded representations of images.

The Perceptron was designed as a physical machine, an analog special-purpose computer that was not programmed but engaged in what was then described as self-organization. The construction of custom hardware to implement this system — a design much more complicated than Rosenblatt's early and simple EPAC computer — would take time and significant funding. The Perceptron would thus have to be initially simulated on a conventional digital computer, an IBM 704, capable of performing the high-precision floating point calculations needed for scientific computing. These were relatively common in scientific computing environments during the late 1950s. Cornell Aeronautical Laboratory had an IBM 704 and they were used by other, similar scientific centers funded by US military and government agencies.

59 Rosenblatt, "Appendix," in "The Perceptron: A Perceiving and Recognizing Automaton."

Demonstrating the Perceptron

On July 7, 1959, Rosenblatt traveled to Suitland, Maryland to visit the United States Weather Bureau (which was renamed the National Weather Service in 1970) to give a public presentation to the national press about his recent work on the Perceptron and to discuss possible applications of this technology. The demonstration was sponsored by the funding agency supporting his work at CAL in Buffalo, the Office of Naval Research (ONR). In 1958 the ONR would spend $40,000 supporting the Perceptron project and, according to the press reports, planned to spend $100,000 in 1959 (almost one million dollars today). These costs were justified through the Cold War context, which necessitated the Defense Department developing advanced computational systems for military surveillance and reconnaissance. There were clear direct military applications for the Perceptron, for tasks ranging from automatic translation to photointerpretation and it was successfully applied to these problems.[60]

Relative to the ONR's announcements, the *Daily Boston Globe* reported that the Navy was "well on the road to developing an electronic robot that could think. It suggested that such devices might be important to the defense of the Western World."[61] Herbert B. Nichols, who covered the event for the *Christian Science Monitor,* also foregrounded the military uses of what he termed a "thinking machine" in his article: "In the face of bold Soviet technological advancements the Perceptron may someday provide answers needed by top United States leaders to swiftly counteract advancements in whatever new channels of discovery the USSR may explore."[62] This positioning of the Perceptron

60 Albert E. Murray, "Perceptron Applicability to Photointerpretation," Phase 1 report for Project PICS, Report VE-1446 G-1 (Cornell Aeronautical Laboratory, 1960), and Albert E. Murray, "Perceptron Applications in Photo Interpretation," *Photogrammetric Engineering* 27, no. 4 (1961): 627–37.

61 "Navy's Going to Build Robot That Can Think," *Daily Boston Globe,* July 8, 1958.

62 Herbert B. Nichols, "Device Expected to 'Think,'" *The Christian Science Monitor,* July 9, 1958.

as a Cold War weapon would continue through the early 1960s. Funding for machine learning and artificial intelligence was dependent upon the imagined uses of such high-technology devices in the virtual arms race with the Soviet Union.

By the early 1970s, the way in which the media reported on Rosenblatt's invention and the visions offered during the Pentagon's announcement surely contributed to the sense that this technology had been oversold and would not be able to deliver on the offered vision of machine learning. The notion that such devices were on track to be automatons would quickly be dismissed and disavowed but at its launch, the learning capacities of the invention were turned into fantasies for the public. The role of training the Perceptron was downplayed and the scenario offered was so simplified that one reporter mistakenly described it as "the first nonbiological system held to be capable of perceiving, recognizing, and identifying external stimuli without any human training or control."[63]

The New York Times reported on this event in an article titled "New Navy Device Learns by Doing: Psychologist Shows Embryo of Computer Designed to Read and Grow Wiser." Their reporting emphasized the future promises of both machine learning and automated production: "Later Perceptrons will be able to recognize people and call out their names and instantly translate speech in one language to speech or writing in another language, it was predicted.... Mr. Rosenblatt said in principle it would be possible to build brains that could reproduce themselves on an assembly line and which would be conscious of their existence."[64] What was actually demonstrated was a linear classification of two distinct patterns made with industry-standard punch cards.

Despite the emphasis and framing of the event as the presentation of a new "device" and a "thinking machine," Rosenblatt's

63 Nichols, "Device Expected to 'Think.'"

64 "New Navy Device Learns by Doing: Psychologist Shows Embryo of Computer Designed to Read and Grow Wiser," *The New York Times*, July 8, 1958, 25, https://www.nytimes.com/1958/07/08/archives/new-navy-device-learns-by-doing-psychologist-shows-embryo-of.html.

demonstration was likely nothing more than a software simulation of the Perceptron demonstrated with the Weather Bureau's IBM 704. This public demonstration was intended to highlight the key features of his Perceptron model by supplying sample input stimuli, a stack of punch cards that had been split into two categories of objects: cards with squares on the left and others with squares on the right. As these cards were inserted into a card reader, the Perceptron simulation program provided feedback on its learning process. Nichols's *Christian Science Monitor* article provided a cogent summary of the demonstration:

> The machine was shown about 100 squares located at random on either the left side or the right side of a rectangular visual field. After viewing these squares, the simulation Perceptron was able to associate one group of squares with "left" and the other group with "right," with 97 per cent consistency in 100 trials. It "learned" to recognize the difference between left and right after it had "seen" only 30 or 40 examples.[65]

This demonstration, although produced in 1958, follows roughly the same protocol used for training and testing machine learning techniques in the twenty-first century. The input stimuli were divided into classes and into a training and testing dataset. As the simulated Perceptron iterated through the input data—which is to say, processed the data item-by-item—it reported on its progress and its accuracy. This was a remarkable demonstration of machine learning but was still a far cry from recognizing speech, thinking, or even processing photographic input. This basic operational procedure is still used today.

In December of 1958, *The New Yorker* published a breezy record of an informal discussion with Frank Rosenblatt, who they describe as passing through New York City on his way to Washington to meet with Marshall C. Yovits, his collaborator and funder at the Office of Navy Research. Addressing Rosenblatt and Yovits as "begetters of the prodigy" recently unveiled

65 Nichols, "Device Expected to 'Think.'"

at the United States Weather Bureau, the author writes, "we conned [Rosenblatt], over a cup of coffee, into a brief exegesis of their brilliant offspring."[66] Rosenblatt explains what he believes to be the significance of his demonstration: "for the first time a non-biological object will achieve an organization of its external environment in a meaningful way." He then explains that Yovits does not share his representation of the Perceptron as a mechanical brain: "my colleague disapproves of all the loose talk one hears nowadays about mechanical brains. He prefers to call our machine a self-organizing system, but, between you and me, that's precisely what any brain is." Yovits had borrowed the term "self-organizing systems" from two researchers at Lincoln Laboratory and would use that name for a conference series he organized on behalf of the Office of Naval Research, which counted Rosenblatt on its roster for its first two conferences in 1960 and 1962.[67]

Despite some disagreement about the naming and framing and also a sense that there were no immediate practical applications of the Perceptron, Rosenblatt was happy to play progenitor. The public discourse of the time was certainly influenced by science fiction that frequently positioned inventors and their creations in parent-child relationships. It was not especially surprising that the relation between Victor Frankenstein and his creation would be invoked by the initial reportage of the Perceptron announcement with the "Shades of Frankenstein!" headline. What was curious was the degree to which Rosenblatt's own research into parent-child relations formed the primary lens through which he himself understood the training of the Perceptron. The operator of the Perceptron, in Rosenblatt's description, was essentially a parent providing positive ("reward") and negative ("punish") reinforcement as the condition

66 Harding Mason, D. Stewart, and Brendan Gill, "Rival," *The New Yorker*, December 6, 1958, 45, https://www.newyorker.com/magazine/1958/12/06/rival-2.

67 Marshall C. Yovits, "Preface," in Marshall C. Yovits, George T. Jacobi, and Gordon T. Goldstein, eds., *Self-Organizing Systems 1962* (Spartan Books, 1962).

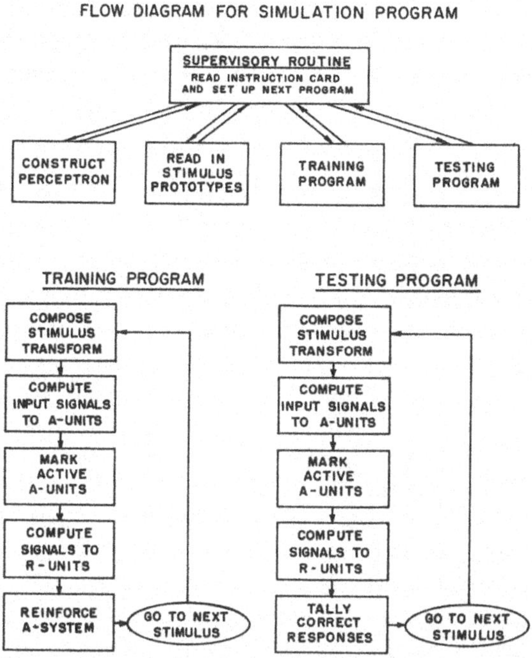

Fig. 2.4. Procedures for Training and Testing a Simulated Perceptron. Rosenblatt, "Perceptron Simulation Experiments," 11.

of learning. It seems, then, that *The New Yorker*'s positioning of Rosenblatt as the father of the Perceptron was a rather fitting characterization.

Design and Operation of a Simulated Perceptron

Rosenblatt's simulation programs — there were many different implementations based on multiple animal-inspired models with multiple architectures and designed for different computers — was inspired by his imagined mechanical device. Even after the creation of multiple physical learning machines, programmers of these simulated devices retained the same nomenclature. The almost parallel procedures used for the training and testing of a simulated Perceptron (see fig. 2.4) reference the marking of units and computing of signals from the virtual equivalents of mechanical devices. The routines also borrowed from psychological studies an experimental paradigm for the observation and evaluation of the programs.

The high level of abstraction and the sophistication of specialized functions and packages in a contemporary programming language like Python makes the simulation of a Perceptron quite simple for us today. When combined with data manipulation packages and standard procedures to test and evaluate machine learning algorithms, a simulated Perceptron can serve as a classification algorithm for many types of problems. The classification of numerical data, especially, is a task well suited to these networks. These data could be sales figures, purchasing history, and pricing used to predict customer behavior (purchase or no purchase). They could be more complex biomedical measurements (lipid panel data, weight, etc.) to predict a patient's status as healthy or unhealthy.

Implementations of a multi-layer Perceptron, a more complex neural network that answers a number of the initial critiques directed toward Rosenblatt's initial formulation, are provided by popular machine learning packages, including scikit-learn. Scikit-learn is a package containing a large collection of high-performance algorithms and tools for machine learning, especially as applied to scientific research. These are used by thousands of researchers and the package comes with thorough documentation, example datasets, and examples of using these methods to solve scientific problems. Walking through a Python implementation of the Perceptron enables us to understand at a slightly more concrete level the conceptual description presented in the previous pages. In the conventional naming scheme used for the variables, we can also see the degree to which the Perceptron is rooted in its material history as an alternative computer design.

The following example uses training data from what is known as the Fisher Iris dataset, a popular sample dataset for machine learning that contains four measurements of fifty samples of three different kind of Iris flowers. This dataset was created by statistician and eugenicist Ronald A. Fisher to support his work on statistical methods for separating samples into taxonomic categories.[68] As the simple version of the Perceptron initially designed by Rosenblatt was only able to discriminate between two categories, we will select only two flower types: the Iris Veriscolor and the Setosa. Each sample has measurements for the sepal and petal width and length. These data are used in the following code to train this simulated Perceptron:

```
import numpy as np
import pandas as pd

# number of training iterations
epochs = 100

# learning rate
eta = 0.01

# read data from local copy of dataset
# https://archive.ics.uci.edu/ml/machine-learning-data-
bases/iris
df = pd.read_csv('iris/iris.data', header=None)

# y: labels for setosa and versicolor
# Iris-setosa == 0
# Iris-versicolor == 1
```

68 Ronald A. Fisher, "The Use of Multiple Measurements in Taxonomic Problems," *Annals of Eugenics* 7, no. 2 (1936): 179–88. Fisher was a eugenicist, as were many other early statisticians, and he published this essay and dataset in a eugenicist academic journal. Much of his work, even outside of his research on population genetics, upheld his racist views and this classification of Iris flowers could be understood within this same eugenicist framework.

```
y = df.iloc[0:100, 4].values
y = np.where(y == 'Iris-setosa', 0, 1)

# Obtain sepal and petal length and widths
# X: four features for each sample
X = df.iloc[0:100, [0,1,2,3]].values

# initialize a set of weights dynamically from data (number
of samples + 1)
# the additional weight is known as the bias
weights = X.shape[1]
weights = np.zeros(weights + 1)

# predict the class 0 or 1 depending on the sum of activa-
tions
def predict(input_data):
    input_data = np.array(input_data)
    weight_sum = np.dot(input_data, weights[1:])
        + weights[0]
if weight_sum > 0:
    activation = 1
else:
    activation = 0
return activation

# train the Perceptron on training data for both classes
# and supply labels (either 0 or 1)
# iterate through each of the training epochs
for e in range(epochs):
    # on each epoch, we update the weights with all the
    training data and labels
    for inputs, label in zip(X, y):
        # predict class and update weights
        prediction = predict(inputs)
        weights[1:] += eta * (label - prediction) * inputs
        weights[0] += eta * (label - prediction)
```

```
# display final weights after training
weights
array([-0.01 , -0.011, -0.036, 0.052, 0.022])

predict([6.8, 3.1, 4.5, 1.2])
1

# sample imaginary data
predict([4.7, 3.0, 1.6, 0.2])
0
```

The Perceptron, as designed by Rosenblatt, is very much a supervised machine learning algorithm. It is supervised because it requires that the training data be labeled correctly by the operator. In binary classification, this generally means either positive or negative examples, which is to say that the program responds with either a 0 (setosa) or 1 (versicolor). Supervision implies an active teacher instructing the machine by presenting samples and correcting the machine (automatically in this case) when it returns an incorrect answer, by comparing the known label to the predicted label and updating the *weights*. Weights are the model's parameters. They are numerical values that are adjusted to "weigh" the different input features. In this toy example, the relative influence of each feature (sepal width, sepal length, petal length, petal width) is adjusted each time data is run through the network. These change independently of each other as data move through the network. It is likely that some features will have greater predictive power than others; for example, it might be the case that the sepal length should have more influence in determining whether a particular flower sample is a setosa or a versicolor. The supervisor or teacher oversees the training procedures and determines the accuracy of the trained model by assessing performance on the testing dataset.

This simulated Perceptron begins with establishing a few parameters. We first determine the number of iterations in which we will present all input data to the Perceptron. Each iteration is called an *epoch* and we set a *threshold* at which point the iterations and updating will be guaranteed to halt. In more advanced versions this can be dynamically altered, or the program can be suspended when the weights are no longer being adjusted and the decision boundary no longer moves. These training epochs allow for what Rosenblatt referred to as the convergence of the Perceptron, the eventual movement of the algorithm toward returning the correct answer to a decision boundary or linear hyperplane that splits the dataset into the pre-established binary categories. The second variable is named *eta* and specifies the learning rate. This variable is used by a Perceptron to adjust the weights by the difference of the returned predicted answer—an answer being the class in binary terms (0=setosa or 1=versicolor) of the sample data—and the correct answer. The value of these two important variables mostly depends on the number of samples, variation found within the samples, and the complexity of the data derived from the samples. Lowering the epoch threshold, which means the data are seen and the weights are adjusted fewer times, might lower the accuracy of the model but also will decrease the amount of time the Perceptron takes to complete its training, leading to faster computation.

The number of weights in this example implementation correspond to the number of features that represent that pattern of each object with the addition of one, the value of what is called the *bias term*. The bias value, like the weights themselves, is adjustable. It is modified during each epoch but unlike the other weights, it does not take the input values into account. The bias term is added to the sum of the other weights to increase accuracy. There are four features that make up what we will call the Iris pattern: sepal length and width and petal length and width. Like the weights, these are stored in a vector, in this instance a simple list of values—for example, [5.1, 3.5, 1.4, 0.2]—that can be operated on simultaneously. The weights, including the bias, are all initialized with the value of zero, [0., 0., 0., 0., 0.], and the values will begin to change as soon as the first prediction is made. A prediction, in this case, would be the return of a binary value (0 for setosa or 1 for versicolor), determined by adding the weights and evaluating if that sum is greater than 0.

If it is greater than 0, then prediction is 1; otherwise, the prediction function returns 0. The known labels that correspond to each vector of features, labeling the entire vector with the correct flower name, are stored in the "y" variable. In this simple Perceptron, these labels are 0 and 1. The next lines of Python code define the prediction function. This returns the predicted response from the activations.

The training function contains two loops, an inner and outer loop. The outer loop simply and repeatedly executes or iterates through the inner loop until the epoch threshold is reached, in this example, one hundred times. This will perform the exact same instructions one hundred times. The inner loop iterates through each training sample and its corresponding label. Each time this loop is executed, it calls the prediction function and obtains a prediction of which of the two categories the supplied data fits into. The weights are then updated by adding to these values the product of *eta,* the learning rate, the difference of the correct label and predicted label, and the input data, the vector of the four features representing each sample.

In the first epoch, when the first prediction is made from the first sample, the weights are all zero. The first prediction determines the product of the weights derived from the features, which are all still zero, and the first sample features and adds to it the value of the additional weight. As the weights are all zero, the first prediction is zero. This turns out to be the correct answer so when the weights are updated, they remain zero. This will not change until the first sample belonging to the second category (the versicolor flowers labeled as 1) is presented. At that point the weights begin to change and the Perceptron moves toward convergence on the correct weights that define the *hyperplane* separating the samples into two classes. The hyperplane is a decision boundary separating the Perceptron's representation of input data into two areas. Think of this as a line slicing through a simple graph, with data representing the setosa flower on one side and the versicolor flower on the other. Using these supplied samples, the Perceptron is trained in three epochs, after which the weights are no longer updated.

If supplied with a linearly separable dataset, even this simple Perceptron will learn to identify the hyperplane that best divides these data into two classes. When used as a linear classifier, this method remains incredibly useful and successful for many applications. While some of the language used to describe the operation of a neural network has changed since Rosenblatt's description of the algorithm, these basic functions of a simulated learning machine are the building blocks of some of the most complex twenty-first-century technologies.

In contemporary machine learning, modular packages are used to design, train, and use neural networks. The PyTorch package bundles together machine learning tools and utilities and is used extensively for deep learning applications.[69] PyTorch is a Python package with native, built-in support for the common data formats used in contemporary machine learning and most importantly, a set of modular tools for constructing neural networks. Larger Multi-Layer Perceptrons (MLPs) are now found in many deep learning networks, including the transformer models used in contemporary Large Language Models (LLMs) and are routinely built using PyTorch or similar packages. The code below implements a version of the above Perceptron with the benefits of contemporary deep learning found in PyTorch, including the automatic adjustment of weights using backpropagation, a more complex loss function designed for classification problems, and an optimizer.

These more sophisticated elements enhance the Perceptron as it was defined in the 1950s and demonstrate how easily it can be brought up to date using contemporary methods. They build on the basic learning algorithm by adding features to enable the construction of larger networks—wider and deeper—and for applications to more complex datasets. Backpropagation, in particular, is an idea that Rosenblatt developed but was not able

69 Adam Paszke et al., "PyTorch: An Imperative Style, High-Performance Deep Learning Library," in *Advances in Neural Information Processing Systems (NeuroIPS)* 32, ed. H. Wallach et al. (Curran Associates, 2019), 8024–35. Documentation and recent code are available at: https://pytorch.org.

to fully implement. In some ways it is another residual technology that was twice rediscovered. In his *Principles of Neurodynamics,* Rosenblatt termed this method the "backpropagating error correction procedure," defining it as the correction of errors found during training procedures and the updating of the values of the neurons through multiple potential layers.[70] Paul Werbos developed a method to make backpropagation work in the 1970s, in his dissertation research, and then later in the 1980s, it was independently implemented by David Rumelhart, Geoffrey Hinton, and Ronald Williams.[71] That later implementation was much better known and was an important stage in the development of neural networks. The following brief code updates the earlier Perceptron example, making use of these contemporary technologies:

```
import numpy as np
import pandas as pd
import torch
import torch.nn as nn

# number of training iterations
epochs = 100

# learning rate
learning_rate = 0.01

# define the Perceptron as three layers: input,
# hidden, output
class Perceptron(nn.Module):
    def __init__(self, input_dim):
        super(Perceptron, self).__init__()
        self.layer1 = nn.Linear(input_dim, 64)
```

70 Rosenblatt, *Principles of Neurodynamics,* 292.

71 Paul Werbos, "Backpropagation: Past and Future," *IEEE International Conference on Neural Networks* 1 (1988): 343–53, and David E Rumelhart, Geoffrey E. Hinton, and Ronald J. Williams, "Learning Representations by Back-Propagating Errors," *Nature* 323 (1986): 533–36.

```
        self.layer2 = nn.Linear(64, 64)
        self.layer3 = nn.Linear(64, 2)

    def forward(self, inputs):
        inputs = torch.relu(self.layer1(inputs))
        inputs = torch.relu(self.layer2(inputs))
        outputs = torch.sigmoid(self.layer3(inputs))
        return outputs

model = Perceptron(input_dim = 4)

# read data from local copy of dataset
# https://archive.ics.uci.edu/ml/machine-learning-data-
bases/iris
df = pd.read_csv('iris/iris.data', header=None)

# y: labels for setosa and versicolor
# Iris-setosa == 0
# Iris-versicolor == 1
y = df.iloc[0:100, 4].values
y = np.where(y == 'Iris-setosa', 0, 1)

# Obtain sepal and petal length and widths
# X: four features for each sample
X = df.iloc[0:100, [0,1,2,3]].values

# convert data and labels to Torch tensor datatype
training_data = torch.FloatTensor(X)
labels = torch.LongTensor(y)

# calculates loss entropy for classification tasks
loss_fn = nn.CrossEntropyLoss()

# the Adam optimizer adjusts weights using
# gradient optimization
optimizer = torch.optim.Adam(model.
        parameters(),lr=learning_rate)
```

```
# train the model
model.train()

# iterate through each of the training epochs
for e in range(epochs):
    model.zero_grad()
    outputs = model(training_data)

    # supply labels (either 0 or 1) to CrossEntropyLoss
    loss_train = loss_fn(outputs, labels)
    loss_train.backward()

    # adjust weights
    optimizer.step()

# define a function to predict class from output
def predict(input_data):
    outputs = model(torch.tensor(input_data))
    pred = torch.argmax(outputs)
    return pred

# sample imaginary data (class 1 or Iris-versicolor)
predict([6.8, 3.1, 4.5, 1.2])
1

# sample imaginary data (class 0 or Iris-setosa)
predict([4.7, 3.0, 1.6, 0.2])
0
```

The Mark I Perceptron: Building the Mechanical Brain

While Rosenblatt's Perceptron was initially a simulation, a software implementation running on an IBM 704 computer, he was keen to construct a dedicated machine that would implement his pattern recognition algorithm. A mechanical Perceptron, a physical machine, would deliver on the promise of an alternative to a general-purpose computer. It would provide a testbed for evaluating an alternative design to the conventional computers that worked more like biological machines.

Rosenblatt's interest in a physical machine was motivated by his desire to have a system that did not simulate neural systems but enacted them, materially. When weights are changed in a simulated Perceptron, the values assigned to variables change; in a mechanical system these changes are registered in analog devices. This rendered the engineering work involved in monitoring these devices more like physiology, like the cognitive neuroscience that was shortly to come. Rosenblatt's Mark I would be dedicated to neural network research, though it would not be the first "learning machine."

In the late 1950s Albert Maurel Uttley created a computer at the National Physical Laboratory in the London suburb of Teddington, England that was a special purpose device modeled on animal learning. Uttley's "conditional probability computer" was inspired by the notion of a conditioned reflex, a behavioralist understanding of learning. Like the neural model, Uttley used the language of activation in response to environmental stimulus. Conditional learning systems could be implemented as mechanical devices — Uttley specifies a hydraulic model that uses liquid in a vessel for counters, an analogue of Rosenblatt's weights — or as an electrical computer. It is not known whether Rosenblatt was aware that his high school classmate and later rival Marvin Minsky had already implemented a much more simplified mechanical learning machine, called the Stochastic Neural Analog Reinforcement Calculator, or SNARC, using Hebb's neural model.[72] Minsky created his learning machine with Dean Edmonds at Harvard in 1951, using motors, three hundred tubes, surplus B24 bomber parts, and forty control knobs that stored the present state of the network. This system did not implement the same decision rule as the one used by Rosenblatt and, outside of some discussion in his doctoral dis-

72 Marvin Minsky, "Theory of Neural-Analog Reinforcement Systems and its Application to the Brain-Model Problem" (PhD diss., Princeton University, 1954).

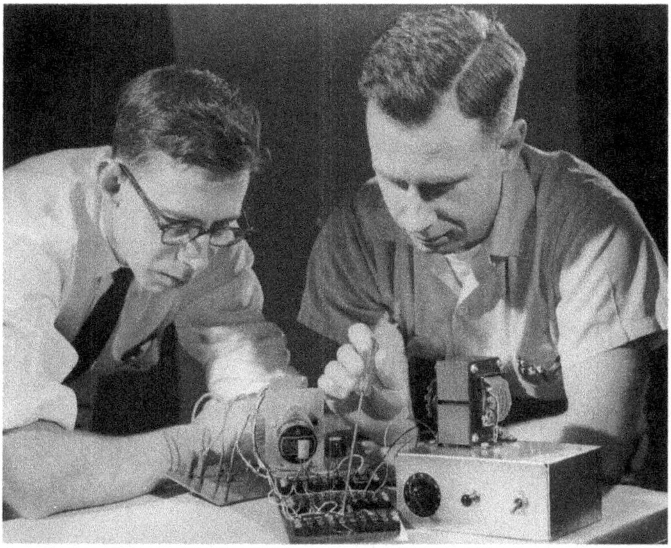

Fig. 2.5. Frank Rosenblatt (left) and Charles W. Wightman (right) working on a prototype association unit for the first Perceptron, December 1958. Courtesy of the Division of Rare and Manuscript Collections, Cornell University Library.

sertation, it was not publicly discussed by Minsky until 1981.[73] This was especially strange because there was considerable enthusiasm for implementing these developing ideas about neural networks as physical machines.

While the Mark I might not have been an automaton, it did materially manifest Rosenblatt's desire to create a physical computing machine. The Mark I was eventually built at Cornell University and today it resides in the Smithsonian Institute, at the National Museum of American History, as a display object under the catalog name of "Neural Network." The machine gave material shape to the Perceptron idea and provided Rosenblatt

73 David E. Rumelhart and David Zipser, "Feature Discovery by Competitive Learning," *Cognitive Science* 9 (1985): 75–112.

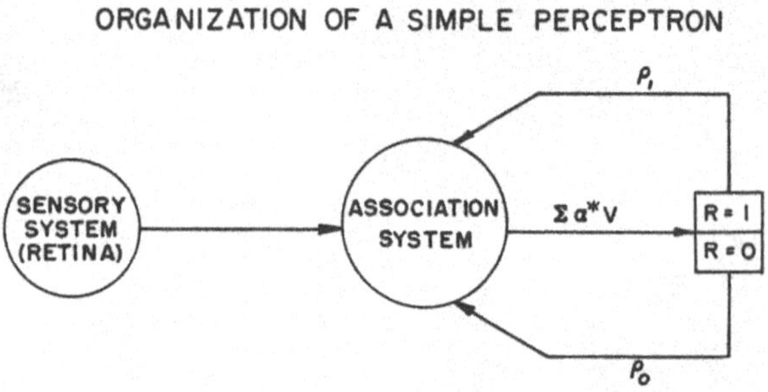

Fig. 2.6. Simple diagram of the Perceptron showing the Sensory (Retina), Association, and Response units. Rosenblatt, "Perceptron Simulation Experiments (Project Para)," 8.

Fig. 2.7. The Mark I Perceptron at the Smithsonian Institute. Courtesy of the Division of Medicine and Science, National Museum of American History, Smithsonian Institution.

with a platform by which to demonstrate the operation of the algorithm. Constructing special purpose hardware for these devices was the norm during the mid-twentieth century. As mentioned above, there were several precursors to the Mark I, including Uttley's conditional probability computer and Minsky's SNARC. These were clunky, small devices that could demonstrate some aspect of learning from input but were far from being able to classify complex data, such as the representations of images used by Rosenblatt. Others, such as Augusto Gamba's PAPA (in English, the Automatic Programmer and Analyzer of Probabilities) and the Stanford MINOS would appear not long after Rosenblatt completed the Mark I.[74] While the Mark I implemented these ideas in hardware, they were first created in software running on a general-purpose computer. This is especially interesting as the design of the algorithm draws on the assumptions that it was hardware. The "connections" established between different "units" were imagined as hardware components before they became implemented in software and then eventually developed as mechanical devices.

The Tobermory

While Rosenblatt's Perceptron model was thought of as a mechanical brain and even wishfully described as an automaton, what Rosenblatt and his students created was an electronic model of a highly simplified biological brain. The "Tobermory" was the second major hardware implementation of the Perceptron algorithm along with new data and sensory acquisition devices. When Rosenblatt first introduced the Perceptron concept, he introduced the photoperceptron as the first implementation

74 On the PAPA system, see Antonio Borsellino and Augusto Gamba, "An Outline of a Mathematical Theory of PAPA," *Il Nuovo Cimento* 20, suppl. 2 (1961): 221–31, and Augusto Gamba, "The Papistor: An Optical PAPA Device," *Il Nuovo Cimento* 26, suppl. 3 (1962): 371–73. The MINOS system is described in Alfred E. Brain et al., "A Large, Self-Contained Learning Machine," in *Proceedings of the Western Electronic Show and Convention* (IEEE, 1963), C-1.

but not before proposing another possible device, "One which accepts tonal patterns, or auditory inputs, will be designated a phonoperceptron, and we might also consider the possibility of electro- or radioperceptrons, with corresponding sensory devices."[75] With its appropriately literary name, the Tobermory was not referred to by Rosenblatt or others as a more generic phonoperceptron (although it was at least once called an audio-perceptron). This project became the subject of George Nagy's doctoral dissertation. Although Nagy was an electrical engineering student at Cornell University, he worked in the Cognitive Systems Research Program (CSRP) and was advised by Rosenblatt. Like all CSRP projects, his work was funded by the Office of Naval Research. Nagy defended his dissertation, "Analogue Memory Mechanisms for Neural Nets," in 1962. In his dissertation, Nagy reviewed the Mark I architecture, its features and shortcomings, and proposed a second-generation system with many improvements.

The Tobermory took its name from the cat in the eponymous short story written by H.H. Monroe, aka "Saki," published in 1911. In Saki's story, during a visit to a large country house, a scientist reveals that he has successfully trained a cat to speak. This cat, Tobermory, was then discovered to have been eavesdropping on private discussions among this group of wealthy individuals and when prompted, reveals all their secrets that he has overheard during the party. The fear of further surveillance and exposure results in a plan to murder Tobermory but he is killed by a neighboring cat first and his body is discovered the following the day.

Saki's story was undoubtedly attractive to Rosenblatt for two reasons, the first being that he greatly liked cats and there were several that lived with him in his farmhouse. The second reason is the inspiration for the design of the machine itself. Building on what Rosenblatt and his colleagues had learned in the design and implementation of the Mark I and in their software imple-

75 Frank Rosenblatt, "The Perceptron: A Perceiving and Recognizing Automaton," 2.

Fig. 2.8. Patch panel components of the Tobermory Perceptron. Image from Frank Rosenblatt's camera, courtesy of William Mutch.

mentations of the Perception, the earlier simplified visual model was replaced in the Tobermory design by a more complex, "feline" animal model.

Rosenblatt's later abstract model of the Perceptron, now described as a neural net, was explicitly designed on the contemporary understanding of a cat's brain. Based on research conducted by David Hubel and Torsten Wiesel of single-cell recordings of cat vision, Rosenblatt and his colleagues developed a new version of his neural network model, initially in the form of a software simulation running on a conventional digital computer.[76] Rosenblatt writes in a description of these more advanced neural networks: "Simulation studies are now in progress which employ a model of the cat's visual cortex, based on the Hubel-Wiesel data, in place of the retina of an elementary perceptron."[77] What the Tobermory, in both its simulated and mechanical versions, added to the original Perceptron was the addition of specialized layers. The additional layers implemented feature detectors. These were designed to recognize higher-level elements. In the case of image data, these would be line and edge detectors. Rosenblatt created four- and five-layer neural networks using this architecture and evaluated them on a variety of data, including images representing alphabetical characters.[78]

In June of 1963 Rosenblatt traveled to an event on learning machines at Northwestern University to present on the Tobermory and could not resist speaking with a reporter. After publishing *Neurodynamics* and working to focus discussions of the Perceptron on its value as a brain model he fell once more into the trap of making predictions about future developments with these machines. While Rosenblatt admitted that the Tobermory was not yet operational, the reporter cites Rosenblatt's predic-

76 David Hubel and Torsten Wiesel, "Receptive Fields, Binocular Interaction and Functional Architecture in the Cat's Visual Cortex," *The Journal of Physiology* 160, no. 1 (1962): 106–54.

77 Rosenblatt, "Analytic Techniques for the Study of Neural Nets," 289.

78 Frank Rosenblatt, "Comparison of a Five-Layer Perceptron with Human Visual Performance," in *Natural Automata and Useful Simulations*, ed. H.H. Patee et al. (Spartan Books, 1963).

tion that "within the next five years it will be possible to build a machine that will perform all the functions of an office secretary and receptionist."

Rosenblatt described some of the limitations of learning machines but continued to offer tantalizing examples of what might be possible with a Perceptron trained to recognize speech. He even offered one highly futuristic prediction: "It will not be long before these machines can be made to hold a conversation.... For example, if you mention the name Polonius, the machine will launch into a discussion of the finer points of Hamlet."[79] Special-purpose computing machines like the Mark I and the Tobermory were expensive and because of their custom design and numerous components, they took a long time to develop and build. While some of these systems may have briefly leapfrogged simulated learning machines on general purpose digital computers, the performance of these much more commonly used systems was increasing at a rapid rate. The greater investment of engineering resources in conventional computing and vastly larger demand for general purpose systems has led to this increase in performance. This, combined with the ease of programming, shifted research and development away from learning machines to machine learning on digital computers. In the present moment, the use of graphics processing units (GPUs) and other specialized hardware for high-speed numerical calculations are greatly speeding up the simulation of neural networks on digital computers. These devices are offloading certain operations — crucially, the many matrix multiplications required for the operation of deep learning neural networks, albeit they remain located within the simulation paradigm.

Rosenblatt's Return to Ithaca

Rosenblatt quickly ascended the research ranks during his time at Cornell Aeronautical Laboratory (CAL). He began as a research

79 Ronald Kotulak, "New Machine Will Type Out What it 'Hears': Can Fill Secretary's Job, Expert Says," *Chicago Tribune*, June 18, 1963.

psychologist and by 1959 was chief of the cognitive systems section, when he returned to Ithaca as the director of the Cognitive Systems Research Program (CSRP) and became a lecturer in the Psychology department. The CSRP was primarily created as an organizational unit for Rosenblatt's Office of Naval Research grant. He started the CSRP from within the Cornell Computing Center before moving to Hollister Hall, with his appointment in Psychology. Rosenblatt moved from his initial research appointment to become a tenured member of the Section of Neurobiology and Behavior in Cornell's Division of Biological Sciences in January of 1966. At this point he moved the CSRP to facilities in Langmuir Laboratory, the institutional home of the Section of Neurobiology and Behavior. He would eventually become acting co-chair of this department, a position he was holding at the time of his death. Rosenblatt used the CSRP to recruit a team of researchers to work with him on Perceptron-related research. The CSRP provided a home and publishing opportunities, in the form of a series of technical reports, for people working on these machines. These reports, which included new work by Rosenblatt, were circulated to a mailing list of approximately one hundred researchers employed at US defense agencies and other sites funded by the Office of Naval Research.

Rosenblatt's return to Cornell University enabled him to teach undergraduates and advise graduate students. He was firmly committed to the transformative possibility of education and worked to ensure that Cornell was welcoming to minorities. In a report he authored as chair of a faculty research committee, Rosenblatt argued that

> [t]he university has a moral obligation to help provide equality of education, equality of educational opportunity, for those who have been deprived of it by virtue of race, poverty, or social circumstances. This includes making potential students aware of the possibility of a university education, making it possible for them to enter, making it feasible for them to stay, economically and socially, and providing stud-

> ies relevant to their needs and interests. This applies to foreign students as well as to Americans.[80]

Rosenblatt had a strong sense of community and his own moral obligations to others. He extended that openness and obligation into some aspects of his personal life. He was known to welcome many undergraduate and graduate students (as well as other young people not enrolled at Cornell University) interested in science and technology into his lab to assist in conducting various research projects. He also invited some of these people into his home.

On July 6, 1961, Rosenblatt purchased a 2,500-square-foot, two-story red brick farmhouse in Brooktondale, an Ithaca suburb, located at 119 Middaugh Road. It was older, dating to 1900, and was in need of some repair and care. An early project undertaken by Rosenblatt and his younger tenants was painting the house white to match the wood clapboard of the attic level. It was situated on thirteen and one-half acres, and when Rosenblatt purchased it, he could see ample space for the construction of new outbuildings (sheds, etc.) and several of his future projects, including the construction of a very large telescope. The rural location gave Rosenblatt some distance from the lights and noise of Ithaca—he had previously lived in the shadow of the university, at 126 College Avenue—and would be an ideal site to build an observatory to house his own high-powered telescope. Over the years Rosenblatt would invite many members of the Cornell community to live with him. After a homemade wine concocted by those living in the house was jokingly called "Chateau Rosenblatt," the nickname stuck. A list of residents and other Chateau Rosenblatt affiliates contains the names of almost sixty individuals with a connection to the house and its community.[81]

80 Frank Rosenblatt, quoted in U.S. Congress, *Congressional Record*, 117th Congress, 21st session, July 28, 1971, H27717.

81 List of residents and affiliates of Chateau Rosenblatt, courtesy of William Mutch. Photograph of typed and handwritten list, June 29, 2022.

Fig. 2.9. Chateau Rosenblatt. Image from Frank Rosenblatt's camera. Courtesy of William Mutch.

Within the context of Cornell University and the late 1960s, this unconventional housing arrangement of a professor living alongside undergraduate and graduate students, dropouts, boyfriends, girlfriends, and random friends of friends is perhaps a little less strange than it might initially appear. What is known as the Telluride House, a Cornell campus residential community, was founded in 1910 and organized as a communal living arrangement that welcomed both faculty and students. The Telluride Association is dedicated to promoting intellectual ac-

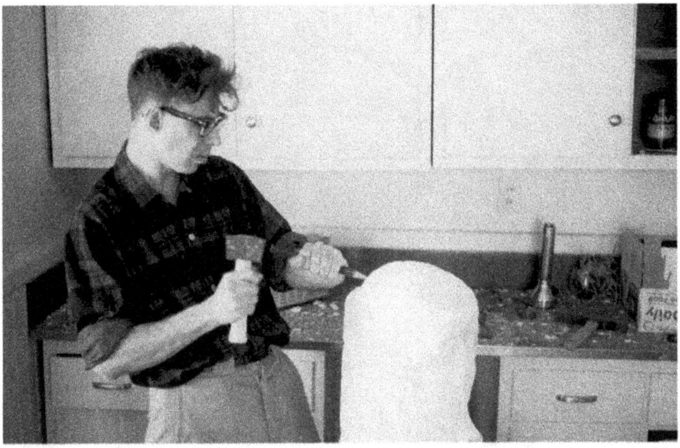

Fig. 2.10. Frank Rosenblatt working on a bust of Rod Miller. Courtesy of William Mutch.

tivities and democratic governance. While the presence of so many young people at Rosenblatt's home might have raised an eyebrow or two, the mixing of faculty and students in existing residential sites like the Telluride House may have provided a precedent. At least two individuals living in Rosenblatt's home, the now very well-known Hal and Eve Sedgwick, had previously lived at Telluride House before moving into the attic of 119 Middaugh Road, showing that there existed some movement between these two communal living spaces.

Eve Sedgwick lists among the residents of Chateau Rosenblatt "kids" who numbered at any given time six to fifteen people: "Rosenblatt's graduate students; old friends; young men who were or had been his lovers; partners, siblings, partners of siblings, and siblings of partners of siblings of the above categories; sometime boys who'd run away from reform school farther upstate. Not counting thirty cats and a dysfunctional blue collie."[82] The widespread interest in the 1960s in alternative so-

82 Michael Moon et al., "Queers in (Single-Family) Space," *Assemblage* 24 (1994): 32–33.

Fig. 2.11. Bust of Rod Miller. Courtesy of Virginia Miller.

cial structures such as communes makes the informal nature of Rosenblatt's home, with people coming and going and sharing in housework and meal preparation, more understandable as a reaction to the normative living arrangements typically found in both the highly nuclear family and Cornell's fraternity system.

Among those living with Rosenblatt was Rodman "Rod" G. Miller, from Montclair, New Jersey. In 1962 during his freshman year at Cornell, Rod met Rosenblatt. After an incident in his first year involving the possession of marijuana resulted in Miller's separation from the university, Rosenblatt provided Rod with faculty support. Over time, Rod would become quite close to Rosenblatt. He was the son of Dr. Helena Miller, a biochemist and clinical research affiliate in the Department of Surgery at Cornell University Medical College (now known as Weill Cornell Medicine) in New York City. Rod, his siblings Amasa and Virginia, and his cousin Philippa would all spend time living at Rosenblatt's home and several of them would join Rod in working for Rosenblatt. Rod and Rosenblatt worked, lived, and traveled together, including a trip to Morocco that was documented by Rosenblatt with a collection of photographs, some of which are included in the first part of this book.

Miller and Rosenblatt co-authored a scientific article, published in the prestigious *Proceedings of the National Academy of Sciences* in 1966, on an experiment to "transfer" learned behaviors from one rat to another by injecting rather crudely extracted brain material taken from rats that had mastered a maze into others.[83] Research in machine learning, artificial intelligence, and computer vision are indebted to animal research.[84] The designs and architectures of most contemporary neural networks, especially convolutional neural networks, are inspired by research conducted on the visual systems of cats and frogs.[85] It is important to note that much of this research irreparably harmed

83 Frank Rosenblatt and Rodman G. Miller, "Behavioral Assay Procedures for Transfer of Learned Behavior by Brain Extracts," *Proceedings of the National Academy of Science* 56, no. 5 (1966): 1423–30.

84 James E. Dobson, "Early Machine Learning and Artificial Animal Intelligences," *Journal of the Midwest Modern Language Association* 57, no. 1 (2024): 63–89.

85 See, especially, Jerome Lettvin et al., "What the Frog's Eye Tells the Frog's Brain," *Proceedings of the IRE* 47, no. 11 (1959): 1940–51, and David H. Hubel and Torsten N. Wiesel, "Receptive Fields, Binocular Interaction and Functional Architecture in the Cat's Visual Cortex," *The Journal of Physiology* 160, no. 1 (1962): 106–54.

animals and resulted in their deaths. This research was deeply unethical, especially those projects without a sound basis in prior findings or those conducted by researchers who were not trained in conducting animal research. In their research, Miller and Rosenblatt made use of artificially constructed mazes and the aforementioned Skinner box to train, condition, and evaluate the rats.

The experience of working closely with Rosenblatt on these animal research projects would become formative for Miller and lead to him pursuing graduate training in the biological sciences. After a one-year separation from the university, Miller graduated from Cornell in 1967. He went to California to pursue additional training and research at the recently founded Salk Institute and he completed a PhD in Biology at the University of California, San Diego in 1976.

Among his many artistic hobbies, Rosenblatt took up sculpting and he carved a large stone bust of Rod Miller. According to those who lived in his home during this time, he was known to work on the bust during stressful times. In his eulogy for Rosenblatt, Rod Miller describes a nightly ritual in which Rosenblatt would read to his gathered community of students and others from a selection of books, including *A Canticle for Liebowitz, Alice in Wonderland, Through the Looking Glass,* and one of his favorites, *The Wind in the Willows.* Miller recalled the moment when he learned that Rosenblatt had died in a sailing accident on his forty-third birthday: "When we found out at the house, somebody sort of summed it up...said that she thought we'd all be dead from cancer, or something else, before Frank, before anything ever happened to Frank, because Frank was the center of so many people's lives, and seemed to be the only stable thing around. And his house was like ... students flowed through it."[86]

In his remarks at the memorial, Miller recalled asking himself, "why Frank didn't have a wife and kids" when "he was a

86 Rodman G. Miller, quoted in U.S. Congress, *Congressional Record,* 117th Congress, 21st session, July 28, 1971, H27717.

Fig. 2.12. Frank Rosenblatt at home in Chateau Rosenblatt. Courtesy of William Mutch.

father to all of us... [and] in a sense we were a father to him"?[87] Rosenblatt would commonly refer to all those living in his house as his "kids" and Miller was not alone in feeling that Rosenblatt's household offered an alternative family during a period (the 1960s & '70s) in which hierarchies were being challenged and students were breaking down traditional social structures. As others would mention, Rosenblatt had affection and even ro-

87 Ibid.

mantic feelings for some of these students and others who lived with him in Ithaca.[88]

Another one of these students was Harold Arthur "Hal" Sedgwick. Like Rosenblatt, Hal had attended Cornell University as an undergraduate, graduating in 1967 before becoming a graduate student in experimental psychology. While an undergraduate, Hal met a high school student by the name of Eve Kosofsky who was visiting Cornell for a summer program. When she later came to the university as an undergraduate, they renewed their friendship. Hal asked Eve out on her eighteenth birthday and the following year they were married.[89] Eve Kosofsky Sedgwick later attended Yale University for graduate study in English literature and went on to become an important figure in literary and gender studies as well as a seminal founding figure in queer theory.

In the summer of 1969, Eve and Hal moved into the attic of Frank Rosenblatt's Brooktondale farmhouse, where they would live until his death. Hal not only lived closely with Rosenblatt, but also worked closely with him, although his doctoral research project went in a slightly different direction than the lines of research followed by Rosenblatt. Hal Sedgwick defended his dissertation, "The Visible Horizon: A Potential Source of Visual Information for the Perception of Size and Distance," in 1973, two years after Rosenblatt's death. Sedgwick was advised by James J. Gibson and references Rosenblatt's first publication in the dissertation, although he makes no reference to the Perceptron research.

Eve Kosofsky Sedgwick, however, *did* refer to Rosenblatt's Perceptron several times in her work, especially in relation to cybernetics and its connections with one of her many intellec-

---

88 In an interview with Rod's brother Amasa Miller, Amasa shared, "I think Frank was in love with my brother." Amasa Miller, interview with James E. Dobson and Rena J. Mosteirin, May 5, 2022.

89 Jane Hu, "Between Us: A Queer Theorist's Devoted Husband and Enduring Legacy," *The New Yorker,* December 9, 2015, https://www.newyorker.com/books/page-turner/between-us-a-queer-theorists-devoted-husband-and-enduring-legacy.

tual pursuits, affect theory. Affect theory, she argued, could find intellectual resources in cybernetic theory. An investment in the resources of early cybernetic thinking was one of the prime currents running through the work of the philosopher Silvan Tomkins and a major influence on Sedgwick's development of affect theory. What Sedgwick, in an essay written with Adam Frank, terms the "cybernetic fold" is situated in between those landmark theoretical frameworks, postmodernism and modernism. In this fold, Sedgwick and Frank find "the early cybernetic notion of the brain as a homogenous, differenti*able* but not originally differentiated system." This potential of the brain animates their thinking about affect and even theory as such, for it enables a rethinking about the relation between structuralism and poststructuralism. Things can start out in one state, say, and become differentiated, even within a structural system. Sedgwick and Frank turn to Rosenblatt's research as the locus for one such machine that might enable them to revitalize systems theory:

> Think of Frank Rosenblatt's Perceptron ... for example, designed in this early moment to teach itself *how to learn* precisely through a process of trial and error. Its theoretical principles went into supposed obsolescence with the emergence of vastly more powerful computers to reemerge only recently under the rubrics of connectionism and parallel distributed processing.[90]

In this account, it wasn't that the Perceptron was limited to a certain class of problems or that more complex methods had yet to be invented in order to build more reliable and larger networks, it was simply a lack of availability of computation. Nonetheless, Sedgwick and Frank see in the Perceptron an idea for a self-learning machine that begins in one state, all zeros, and over time becomes composed of differentiated units. The trans-

90 Eve Kosofsky Sedgwick and Adam Frank, "Shame in the Cybernetic Fold: Reading Silvan Tomkins," in *Touching Feeling: Affect, Pedagogy, Performativity,* by Eve Kosofsky Sedgwick (Duke University Press, 2003), 107.

formation happens without intention, because of changes in responses to data moving through the network. Casting themselves as operators of a Perceptron-like system, Sedwick and Frank sought to revitalize critique by "observing the automatic nervous system" of theory and noting the changing states and their potentialities.[91]

Sedgwick's work in queer theory also shows important influences from her time living with Rosenblatt. A biography of Sedgwick makes the claim that "the Brooktondale community was a formative model for Sedgwick's conception of the non-nuclear, non-biological family, as Frank Rosenblatt was one of her models of the bachelor 'uncle.'"[92] As part of her critical account of queer theory, Sedgwick interrogated compulsory heterosexuality and the dominance of the nuclear family through the investigation of nonreproductive and nonconforming individuals and their relations to others. The "avuncular" is a key concept in Sedgwick's repertoire and in an essay titled "Tales of the Avunculate: Queer Tutelage in *The Importance of Being Earnest*," she argues that these figures and what they represent provide important models, even within the larger family structure, for queer people: "We are many, the queer women and men whose first sense of the possibility of alternative life trajectories came to us from our uncles and aunts —even when the stories we were allowed to hear about their lives were almost unrecognizably mangled, often in demeaning ways, by the heterosexist hygiene of childrearing."[93] Rosenblatt's influence on the students and others in his alternative and nonconforming Chateau Rosenblatt family thus might have extended to provide a sense of a different way of living and a different relation to relationality. "'Uncle,'" Sedgwick explains, "is very different, *not*

91 Ibid., 117.

92 T. Meyerhoff, Sarah McCarry, and Hal Sedgwick, "Life of Eve Kosofsky Sedgwick," *Eve Kosofsky Sedgwick*, https://evekosofskysedgwick.net/biography/biography.html.

93 Eve Kosofsky Sedgwick, "Tales of the Avunculate: Queer Tutelage in *The Importance of Being Earnest*," in *Tendencies* (Duke University Press, 1993), 63.

a persona or type but a relation, relying on a pederastic/pedagogical model of male filiation to which also, as we have seen, the modern rationalized inversion and 'homo-' models answer only incompletely and very distortingly."[94]

If one reads Rosenblatt as a figure of an "alternative life" trajectory, his early loss, the cutting short of this trajectory, would be a traumatic event. In *A Dialogue on Love,* Sedgwick described the impact of his death on her and the other residents of the house in such terms: "It was a commune where [Rosenblatt] was the kind of absent-minded-scientist daddy. [His death] was the very most shocking, the most completely out of the blue, and he was someone we loved who was also a central person in our everyday lives. There's a way that after that I never stopped knowing how abruptly absolutely anything could be lost."[95]

Sedgwick would explore some of these feelings of absolute loss in a reflective poem she wrote following Rosenblatt's death, titled "A Death by Water":

> There was a real death on a real summer night.
> I rocked and rocked, to offer the death, room and time,
> but it had taken its own time and contracted its own room
> and was really gone.
> I was so adequate on that chair,
> so naked, compact, inexorable, and rich.
> I worked. I was all there.
> Not dead in struggle like a fish.
> It will not be borne — I want to say — we are lost.
> I want to rock this death out, but it's already
> out: it is bearable. But at the usual cost.
> This world has rocked me badly.[96]

---

94 Ibid., 60.

95 Eve Kosofsky Sedgwick, *A Dialogue on Love* (Beacon Press, 1999), 63.

96 Eve Kosofsky Sedgwick, "A Death by Water (1969-1971)," in *Bathroom Songs: Eve Kosofsky Sedgwick as a Poet,* ed. Jason Edwards (punctum books, 2017), 246.

For Sedgwick, these experiences would be formative. Living at Rosenblatt's home gave her a functional and loving model of alternative modes of living and family arrangements. "Looking back," she writes, "I can't disentangle the loveliness of the space, the miasma of my depression, the delight and pathos of this quintessential stage for 'kids amusing ourselves.'"[97] Sedgwick's sense of loss was shared by the other residents of the house. "Rocked" by his death, some of the residents turned the house into a virtual living museum, leaving Rosenblatt's possessions intact, and continued their communal living project with the support of Maurice Rosenblatt.

Frank Rosenblatt received and preserved much of his correspondence, especially letters from students and other young friends.[98] As yet another marker of his relative obscurity and disappearance from public view, these materials ended up in Maurice Rosenblatt's archive at the Library of Congress. While Frank predeceased Maurice by many years, the presence of these materials in Maurice's collection demonstrates the degree to which he was deemed the more notable Rosenblatt. Frank Rosenblatt's archive of materials, a small set of folders, is almost entirely one-sided, consisting of a handful of letters — formal and informal — and postcards sent to Rosenblatt between his high school years and shortly before his death. Many of the letters are addressed to "Dr. Rosenblatt," a form of address that signal a deep respect for their recipient, yet their contents often reveal a surprising degree of intimacy and personal detail, producing an intriguing tension between formality and informality. Rosenblatt's correspondents describe struggles with mental health (several mention depression or mood disorders), challenges in dating and family relationships, academic and professional experiences, and memories of Brooktondale or Ithaca. In March 1968, he received a letter from one young man request-

97 Moon et al., "Queers in (Single-Family) Space," 33.

98 These undigitized materials can be found in the Library of Congress. Maurice Rosenblatt papers, 1910–2003 (bulk 1942–2000), Box II:18, Part II: Frank Rosenblatt Papers, 1943–1971. Personal correspondence, 1943–1945, 1961–1971, undated (7 folders). Library of Congress, Washington, DC.

Fig. 2.13. Frank Rosenblatt's dog Disraeli awaiting his return after his death. Image courtesy of William Mutch.

ing support for a claim to conscientious objector status vis a vis the Vietnam War, to be submitted to a draft board. Some letters even contain declarations of romantic love. This complexity points to the nature of Rosenblatt's relationships, which were often intergenerational friendships marked by mentorship and emotional connections that often coalesced into what today would be called queer kinship.[99]

99 See the essays collected in Tyler Bradway and Elizabeth Freeman, eds., *Queer Kinship: Race, Sex, Belonging, Form* (Duke University Press, 2022).

Among the archive's contents are traces of Rosenblatt's efforts to assist a young woman in securing a job with a colleague in England who was also researching learning machines. Later correspondence includes a request for a letter of recommendation from Rosenblatt, to be submitted as background information in support of the woman's decision to place her recently born child up for adoption at an agency in Cambridge, England. Many of the saved letters also document Rod Miller's movements as he traveled across the country, visiting friends and family. Within Rosenblatt's network of correspondents, Miller serves as a central node, connecting writers and prompting updates. Throughout these letters, the enduring influence of Rosenblatt's presence on a serendipitous constellation of friendships becomes unmistakably clear.

The First AI Winter and a Revolution in Thinking

The initial public unveiling of the yet-to-be-built Perceptron represented a post–World War II military fantasy. It was described as an automaton well before such technology existed. It was hyped and sold to the military and the American public as a revolutionary technology. As the Cornell Aeronautical Laboratory proposal claims, the Perceptron was intended to be a perceptual automaton with the ability to solve military intelligence problems, later explicitly connected to the problem of photointerpretation: the automatic analysis of aerial reconnaissance images.[100] It was an exciting new idea and would eventually become materialized in hardware, although far from an automaton.

In many ways it was inevitable that the Perceptron would fail to deliver on its promises. It was a simulation of a simulation. The target, a biological model of perception based on simplistic mathematical descriptions and research findings drawn from animal experimentation, is incredibly complex and the technology to automatically recognize objects from image data remains

100 Murray, "Perceptron Applications in Photo Interpretation."

at present challenging and fraught with both technical and social problems. These many challenges include difficulties related to image ontology; the frequently ambiguous relation between foreground and background objects; the need to update models for new images and categories; and the selection and naming of possible images to serve as training data for classification.

Two events occurred in the tumultuous year of 1969 to slow progress on artificial intelligence, machine learning, and the Perceptron. Rosenblatt had already begun to shift his research interests in other directions — such as with the above-mentioned research into the transfer of learning by moving cells from one rat's brain to another in the mid-1960s — but these two events significantly cooled the support and enthusiasm for research into these areas. The "cooling" metaphor has been widely used to characterize both this moment and a later moment in the 1980s as "AI winters."

The first major event was the publication of Marvin Minsky and Seymour Papert's *Perceptrons* (1969).[101] The appearance of this book — dedicated to Minsky's Bronx Science classmate Frank Rosenblatt — is considered by many as the primary event that determined the fate of the Perceptron and artificial intelligence research in general, at that time. Minsky and Rosenblatt were known to frequently debate each other at conferences. Pamela McCorduck notes that "[many] in computing remember as great spectator sport the quarrels Minsky and Rosenblatt had on the platforms of scientific conferences during the late 1950s and early 1960s."[102] The critique, in published form, began in Minsky's 1961 review of extant work in the field of artificial intelligence. In this review, Minsky observes that the "'perceptron' class of machines have facilities neither for obtaining better-than-chance properties nor for assembling better-than-additive combinations of those it gets from random construction."[103]

101 Marvin Minsky and Seymour Papert, *Perceptrons: An Introduction to Computational Geometry* (MIT Press, 1969).

102 McCorduck, *Machines Who Think*, 106.

103 Marvin Minsky, "Steps Toward Artificial Intelligence," *Proceedings of the IRE* 49, no. 1 (1961): 15.

In essence, Minsky claims, based on his analysis of the initial 1958-era Perceptron, such neural networks will not be able to classify data at an accuracy rate higher than 50% or "chance," meaning the flip of a coin. Minsky and Papert's *Perceptrons* was a dedicated treatment of the theory of computation through the class of machine learning algorithms that followed Rosenblatt's basic design. It is simultaneously a quirky and academically rigorous book. Signaling their engineering training, Minsky and Papert number their chapters beginning with 0 rather than 1. The book features many hand-drawn figures and handwritten passages, including their dedication to Rosenblatt, added to the second edition after his death. It is also filled with mathematical proofs that demonstrate some significant limitations for single-layer linear machine-learning algorithms. Minsky and Papert continue to address only the simplest of neural networks in their book; as the preceding pages have shown, Rosenblatt had developed and published research on many different neural network architectures, including four- and five-layer networks and cross-coupled systems. This work had been published in the early 1960s and was available to Minsky and Papert, yet they decided to continue to focus just on the simple networks and group all work on neural networks under this category in order to dismiss the entire project:

> Our discussion will include some rather sharp criticisms of earlier work in this area. Perceptrons have been widely publicized as "pattern recognition" or "learning" machines and as such have been discussed in a large number of books, journal articles, and voluminous "reports." Most of this writing (some exceptions are mentioned in our bibliography) is without scientific value and we will not usually refer by name to the works we criticize. The sciences of computation and cybernetics began, and it seems quite rightly so, with a certain flourish of romanticism. They were laden with attractive and exciting new ideas which have already borne rich fruit. Heavy demands of rigor and caution could have held this development to a much slower pace; only the

> future could tell which directions were to be the best. We feel, in fact, that the solemn experts who most complained about the "exaggerated claims" of the cybernetic enthusiasts were, in the balance, much more in the wrong. But now the time has come for maturity, and this requires us to match our speculative enterprise with equally imaginative standards of criticism.[104]

Despite presenting their work as offering a mature and rigorous critique, the great reduction and simplification of neural networks did a disservice to the field and to Rosenblatt. While Rosenblatt, unlike others working on these technologies at the time, was mentioned by name, the publication of *Perceptrons* in effect produced the same sense of erasure that consigned these researchers to the dustbin of computer history. The strongly worded claim that much of this work was "without scientific value" was damning.

The sense of scientific consensus produced by Minsky and Papert lingered over the legacy of Rosenblatt and neural network research for a long time. Cornell's Richard O'Brien, who was the founder and director of the university's Division of Biological Sciences during Rosenblatt's tenure, said of Rosenblatt's Perceptron research that, "for years, he wrote and researched this whole area of artificial intelligence, and we still don't know whether in fact he was on the right track, or whether it was a false track."[105] O'Brien voiced the suspicions of many at the time. It would be decades before we learned that Rosenblatt was indeed on the right track. While it had its limitations — when used for images, the original Perceptron implementation required that all images were size- and position-normalized — these early experiments were successful and the Perceptron and related models were put to use for numerous data classification tasks. It was not uncommon, in the following decades, for many to assume that the Per-

104 Minsky and Papert, *Perceptrons*, 4.

105 Richard O'Brien, quoted in U.S. Congress, *Congressional Record*, 117th Congress, 21st session, July 28, 1971, H27717.

ceptron did not work, that it was too limited, or that the only model Rosenblatt had designed or imagined was a single-layer network. Much of that sense was shaped by Minksy and Papert but also by early field histories, such as Pamela McCorduck's *Machines Who Think*. Today's most sophisticated deep learning neural networks are based on Rosenblatt's research and have been seen as incredibly powerful tools for processing data. They have, in fact, now been recognized for their particular success in the areas of speech and image recognition that were originally targeted by Rosenblatt.

The second major event was the passage of the Mansfield Amendment. Almost the entirely of Rosenblatt's research at Cornell Aeronautical Laboratory and Cornell University was funded by the US military. The US Navy sponsored his initial research and Rosenblatt and his colleagues held contracts from several different government agencies and organizations. The Mansfield Amendment was introduced by Senator Mike Mansfield of Wisconsin, a Democrat, in late 1969. Passed as part of the 1970 Military Authorization Act (Public Law 91-121), this amendment required that all research supported by the military have a direct military application. The Defense Department could no longer fund projects that supported basic "pure" research. "None of the funds authorized by this Act," the amendment states, "may be used to carry out any research project or study unless such project or study has a direct and apparent relationship to a specific military function." While Rosenblatt's Perceptron project started out with an explicit military application — the automation of the photointerpretation of aerial reconnaissance images of military interest — his research had shifted away from this direct application to basic research on neural networks, especially through his framing of them as brain models, and other work on learning. Rosenblatt's colleagues called him a "victim" of this change in funding priorities, stating that, after a period of having hundreds of thousands of dollars annually to advance his research agenda, "within a few

Fig. 2.14. Frank Rosenblatt constructing his backyard observatory. Image from Frank Rosenblatt's camera, courtesy of William Mutch.

years that money melted like summer snow and soon he had very little left the last few months."[106]

At the time of Rosenblatt's death, the Perceptron seemed to many observers and colleagues to be just one of several other exciting ideas that had captivated him and yet were ultimately fruitless. His studies based on animal model research, especially those involving the transfer of learned behavior, did not produce reliable results and were deeply ethically suspect—especially for someone, like Rosenblatt, who had a great affection for animals. His research in astronomy had resulted in publications and while he did have the support of colleagues, including Carl Sagan, Cornell was not supportive of this research, leading him to conduct his studies with the telescope in the observatory that he built in his own backyard.

Rosenblatt's turn to his own backyard provides a compelling metaphor for understanding a political turn that was slow in coming but would produce something of a new conscience for

106 Ibid.

Rosenblatt, one that was just beginning to redefine the meaning of his past and present entanglements in US military-funded research at the time of his death. The events of the late sixties, especially the United States' ongoing involvement in the Vietnam War and the contentiously violent 1968 Democratic National Convention in Chicago, Illinois, served to produce something of a revolution in Rosenblatt's politics and the relationship between these and his research projects.

In the late 1950s and early 1960s Rosenblatt did not appear to have a problem positioning the Perceptron as a weapon in the Cold War and proposing the use of his invention for aerial surveillance tasks. While the decline in available funding from US government agencies and the military synced with his gradual turning away from Perceptron-related research in favor of other projects, his growing political awareness appeared to be connected to a sense that the products of his prior research were now being used as weapons in a war that he opposed. He was fully aware that the Mark I was being used to locate targets of military interest by the US Navy and the CIA.

Rosenblatt thus underwent a political turn that enabled him to connect his liberal politics, which were becoming explicitly anti-war, with his research in machine learning and perception. After leaving CAL for Cornell, Rosenblatt continued to be funded by the US Department of Defense agencies. At least until 1969, Cornell University only supplied fifty percent of Rosenblatt's salary, with thirty percent coming from the Office of Naval Research.

In the early 1960s, he communicated several times with US intelligence agencies. Rosenblatt does not appear to have worked for the CIA, but he was in contact with the agency and several times provided copies of correspondence and reports to them. In April of 1961, he provided a report to Perry Ross, a CIA agent working out of Syracuse, New York, on Rosenblatt's sense of the state of neural network research in the USSR. Rosenblatt based his report on conversations he had with a Soviet researcher named A.V. Napolkov at an academic conference in Karlsruhe, Germany. He ends his report speculating that "the state of the art is actually considerably behind what it is here."[107] Perry Ross was well known and communicated with other Cornell faculty about their research and international travel; while Rosenblatt's available communications are mostly technical reports and letters describing progress with machine learning, he appears to have ended his relationship with the CIA by the mid-1960s.[108]

The campus-wide opposition to CAL's military contracts, which in addition to computer vision and machine learning research also included work on chemical and biological warfare agents like napalm, was intensifying in the late 1960s. This same student-driven anti-war protest activity was taking place at other institutions with military-funded research laboratories, including MIT, which ran the MITRE laboratory, and Stanford University, which operated the Stanford Research Institute. Both labs were involved in developing technology and weapons systems for the Department of Defense.[109] There was significant debate and protest at universities hosting such research facilities. In October of 1967, the *Cornell Daily Sun*, the campus student newspaper, covered the ongoing debate over the relation between CAL and Cornell University. A number of students had demanded the immediate separation of CAL and were opposed by some members of the faculty, especially those with research appointments or collaborators at CAL. While CAL was not close

107 Frank Rosenblatt, "Report on Discussions with A.V. Napolkov, at NTG Conference at Karlsruhe, April 1961," Letter to Perry Ross, May 20, 1961. In Box 18, Folder 7: Maurice Rosenblatt papers, 1910–2003 (bulk 1942–2000), Box II:18, Part II: Frank Rosenblatt Papers, 1943–1971. Personal correspondence, 1943–1945, 1961–1971, undated (7 folders). Library of Congress, Washington, DC.

108 Perry Ross is identified as a CIA agent visiting campus to talk with faculty in an article published in the Cornell student newspaper: Sam Roberts, "Faculty Reveals CIA Sessions," *Cornell Daily Sun*, March 8, 1967.

109 On the military reconnaissance and weapons research conducted at these sites, see Sarah Bridger, *Scientists at War: The Ethics of Cold War Weapons Research* (Harvard University Press, 2015), Stuart W. Leslie, *The Cold War and American Science: The Military-Industrial-Academic Complex at MIT and Stanford* (Columbia University Press, 1994), and Kent C. Redmond and Thomas M. Smith, *From Whirlwind to MITRE: The R&D Story of The SAGE Air Defense Computer* (MIT Press, 2000).

to the Cornell University campus — Buffalo and Ithaca are separated by approximately one hundred and fifty miles — students at Cornell and elsewhere wanted to distance universities from the military. The faculty was poised to vote on the issue again after voting to preserve the existing relationship with CAL the previous year. The newspaper's coverage included a "pro" and "con" feature, with Rosenblatt on the side of the university divesting from CAL and Franklin K. Moore, a member of the engineering faculty, taking the opposing position. Both had previously worked at CAL and held administrative positions at the laboratory.

Rosenblatt's argument, at this time, was not linked to the specific research activities of the Lab or even political motivation; rather, he saw CAL as not contributing to the university and perhaps being better aligned with other academic institutions: "Based on his experiences at CAL, Rosenblatt says, 'For quite some time the people at CAL have thought that they would be better off without Cornell'.... He says that one possibility for severing relations with CAL is a proposal to allow CAL to give research opportunities to all colleges in the area, not solely Cornell."[110] This was not in response to CAL's politics — to their work in support of the US Defense Department, military activities in Vietnam, or their ties to the CIA. Rosenblatt's opinion that CAL should be separated from the university was shared with the students and the editorial board of the Cornell Daily Sun, although their stance was much more politically motivated. The students noted the recent exposure of CAL's work supporting counter-insurgency programs in Thailand and argued that "[t]he role of a university and of an institute conducting questionable research are irreconcilable. The former endeavors to promote intellectual excellence through free and open discussion of academic problems. The latter seeks to further the interests of a few, within a closed, secretive chamber."[111] In an official

110 Deborah Huffman, "Faculty Confrontation: Vote on CAL Expected Today," *Cornell Daily Sun*, October 11, 1967.

111 Ibid.

history on their website, the Calspan Corporation describes the separation as due to the "lack of significant interaction between the University and the Laboratory."[112]

Rosenblatt would soon become involved in Democratic Senator Eugene McCarthy's presidential campaign. He began locally, in December of 1967, by circulating to fellow Cornell faculty a request for signatures on a position statement he had written endorsing McCarthy. He had support from many of his colleagues for this group statement. In a letter on English department letterhead, Arthur Mizener wrote:

> Thanks for the copy of "our" statement. It seems to me excellent of its kind: it says something precise without, I think, saying anything a large number of people like us won't agree with. The problem with these statements is that everybody wants to rewrite them — especially with respect to insignificant details [a vice particularly widespread among *English* professors]. I think you did a marvelous job here. I am particularly impressed by the subtlety of "We see in Senator McCarthy a rallying point for the beginning of genuine change"; just what he is, I think. Anyhow, thanks very much for including me in this operation.[113]

Others, such as Andrew Hacker, a professor in the Department of Government, informed Rosenblatt that they would not sign and in the case of Hacker, he supported McCarthy's opponent: "permit me to add that while you are expending your energies on this futile exercise, I am working hard to nominate a Republican who will not only defeat your Party's Lyndon Johnson in November but who will better accomplish most of the goals that

112 Calspan Corporation, "Fact Sheet," 2005, archived at https://web.archive.org/web/20060321051040/http://www.carsafety.com/history.htm.

113 Arthur Mizener, Letter to Frank Rosenblatt, December 12, 1967. In Box 18, Folder 10, Maurice Rosenblatt papers, 1910–2003 (bulk 1942–2000), Box II:18, Part II: Frank Rosenblatt Papers, 1943–1971. Personal correspondence, 1943–1945, 1961–1971, undated (7 folders). Library of Congress, Washington, DC.

you have in mind." Rosenblatt later traveled to New Hampshire and California to support McCarthy's primary activities. McCarthy's anti-war position was of the utmost importance to Rosenblatt and others in his circle, especially those who had been subject to the draft.

In his remarks delivered at Rosenblatt's memorial, David Connor writes of 1968 as a conversion moment for Rosenblatt that brought him to support Eugene McCarthy's presidential campaign:

> One of the most imprudent things that Frank ever did happened in 1968, when he interrupted his life for three months because he saw a vision, because a man inspired him, gave him a hope, that there could be indeed a moral politics, there could be in the dearth of charismatic and insightful leadership, someone who the people could call to authority and to power. So he set aside his research, his teaching; he set aside many of his own needs, to go from New Hampshire to California and to put his particular insights and talents to use. So that that charismatic man could lead the people of this country away from the death and destruction, the racism and the hatred.[114]

Rosenblatt went to Chicago in August of 1968 for the Democratic National Convention and loaned $1,000 of his own money to the McCarthy campaign to print a booklet titled "Lose or Win," authored by Gerald Hill, who was, just like McCarthy and Rosenblatt, an academic. The students and others in Rosenblatt's circle were also becoming increasingly political and involved in liberal politics and McCarthy's campaign. Rod Miller, who had left Ithaca for California and was working in a lab at the Salk Institute at the time, also went to Chicago for the Democratic National Convention. Miller left, like many other young people,

114 David Connor quoted in U.S. Congress, *Congressional Record,* 117th Congress, 21st session, July 28, 1971, H27717.

with a deep pessimism for electoral politics and an enduring sense of loss and discouragement.

The Office of Naval Research Contract, Nor 401-40, was officially terminated in 1971. In March of that year, just a few short months before his death, Rosenblatt issued his final summary report on his activities that had been supported by ONR during the previous twelve years. He issued the report on behalf of the activities of the Cognitive Systems Research Program rather than his individual research projects, which enabled him to include the research of twelve doctoral students and two master's degree students, and a number of his collaborators in other departments and universities. Rosenblatt used this final report to synthesize what others had seen as disconnected and unrelated projects. Under the broad umbrella of intelligent systems, he included mathematical and theoretical work, the simulation of neural networks, the development of specialized hardware platforms, his physiological and behavioral studies involving rats and cats, and his astronomical research. While listed as one area among others, the simulation work in the form of digital computer programming provided connective links to the other projects: "[A] variety of conventional digital computation programs have also been completed, to aid in theoretical analyses and provide numerical examples where required. Extensive use has also been made of digital computation for statistical data processing in connection with the biological and behavioral experiments described below."[115] Rosenblatt's short, four-page report provides brief summaries of these activities and has some forward-looking statements about future projects and works in progress, but essentially considers the program complete.

Beginning in 1970, Rosenblatt began spending a considerable amount of time in Washington with colleagues from Cornell who were working together as part of The Air War Study Group, a research group supported by the university's Program

115 Frank Rosenblatt, "Final Summary Report on Contract Nor 401-40: Cognitive Systems Research Program," *Office of Naval Research,* March 1971, https://apps.dtic.mil/sti/pdfs/AD0720416.pdf.

on Peace Studies. Cornell's group, like those found at other universities, including Stanford's Biology Study Group, sought to use their specialized academic expertise to influence US policy and public opinion through publication and protest. The Air War Study Group was composed of twenty diverse individuals. Two were affiliated with institutions other than Cornell. There were two undergraduate students, several graduate students, and faculty from several different departments, including the well-known astronomer Carl Sagan, who had recently come to Cornell after being denied tenure at Harvard University in 1968. They went to research, advocate, and lobby for anti-war policies, especially the Hatfield-McGovern amendment to the 1970 appropriations bill that called for the withdrawal of US military troops from Vietnam by the end of 1971, which was defeated on September 1, 1970. The group's research resulted in the publication of a detailed and comprehensive report published on November 8, 1971 under the title of *The Air War in Indochina.* The report was edited by Raphael Littauer and Norman Uphoff, two of Rosenblatt's Cornell colleagues, and opens with a dedication to Rosenblatt: "We dedicate this report to the memory of Frank Rosenblatt whose enthusiasm did much to launch the Study Group and whose unstinting work contributed greatly to our progress. He died in a boating accident on July 11, 1971."

Rosenblatt began his career as a graduate student developing methods to understand the visual perception mechanisms of Air Force pilots. A chance encounter with James J. Gibson, as previously mentioned, resulted in Rosenblatt contributing to the mathematical modeling of environmental perception, the embedded perspective of a pilot attempting to remap spatial relations, between the air and ground, during the landing of a plane. He went on to the creation of machines and algorithms, funded by the Office of Naval Research, for the photointerpretation of military reconnaissance images. So much of his research was concerned with the perspective of military aircraft, from the embodied perspective of the pilot to the top-down view of the aerial photointerpreter. These tasks and positions informed his understanding of the environment in which machine learning would operate. These experiences, those positive and negative examples seen during his and others' experiments with the Perceptron, informed his later participation as a concerned member of the Cornell University community in the creation of a damning account of American military policy in Vietnam.

This group of students and faculty spent the summer of 1970 in Washington, DC, conducting research that was eventually published in book form as *The Air War in Indochina.*[116] Prior to the start of this research session, Rosenblatt told university reporters that as part of the project, "we'll be working to support the Hatfield-McGovern amendment, and with another group coordinating efforts for the November elections.[117] *The Air War in Indochina* singles out the use and indeed the dependency upon advanced military technology—technologies increasingly reliant upon the perceptual technologies created by Rosenblatt and further developed by his colleagues at Cornell Aeronautical Laboratory/Calspan Corporation—as the largest area of concern. The report notes both the lack of accuracy in using computer-assisted technology to identify targets, as "indiscriminate devastation" and the mismatch between the supposed goal of this kind of reconnaissance with the reality of the war. In commenting on what the authors present on the widespread assumption that "mechanized firepower is America's greatest strength," they argue that

> this is doubtless what the developers of the *electronic battlefield* have in mind—making airpower more specific in its counterinsurgency capabilities. However, the primary assumption—that an insurgency can be tackled remotely by the deployment of firepower—remains unchallenged. It appears to us that the step toward automated warfare is in this context a step backward, not forward.[118]

116 Air War Study Group, *The Air War in Indochina,* ed. Raphael Littauer and Norman Liphoff, rev. ed. (Beacon Press, 1971).
117 Frank Rosenblatt, quoted in "C.U. Anti-War Group Lobbying in D.C.," *Cornell Chronicle* 1, no. 30 (May 14, 1970), 15.
118 Air War Study Group, *The Air War in Indochina,* 190n22.

The report's concluding paragraph addresses these technologies specifically and their central role in facilitating what it calls the "failure of the American imagination":

> the very availability of an advanced technology tends to inhibit the imagination. If powerful tools are at hand, it is almost a reflex to reach for them first: and how much greater the temptation to do so if the cost is relatively low. The Nixon Doctrine, Vietnamization, and the evolution of the electronic battlefield and automated warfare, all place growing emphasis on the technology of air warfare as a handmaiden to a set of policy aims which, with lesser though still awesomely powerful means of implementation, have shown themselves elusive and costly. The experience with air warfare in Indochina suggests that a reassessment of American policy there is long overdue.[119]

It is not clear how Rosenblatt understood the implication of his changing politics in relation to his research, its funders, and the eventual application of his inventions, nor do we have a sense of the degree to which he felt, as an engineer and researcher, complicit in the ongoing air war and other uses of these technologies. Rosenblatt unfortunately left few personal writings behind. The strongest sense we can get of his shifting political commitments are from his activities supporting Eugene McCarthy, his defense of international students at Cornell invoked above in the context of his report, as chair of a summer committee on the relationship of the university to minority groups, and his participation in Cornell's Air War Study Group.[120]

119 Ibid., 193.
120 Richard O'Brien, quoted in U.S. Congress, *Congressional Record,* 117th Congress, 21st session, July 28, 1971, H27717.

Rosenblatt's Tragic End

Rosenblatt's many intense interests and his love of the *Wind in the Willows* earned him the nickname "Mr. Toad." His somewhat impulsive purchase of a 41-foot wooden sailboat painted blue that he named the *Shearwater* provides an excellent example of this aspect of his character. Like Kenneth Grahame's Mr. Toad, Rosenblatt was the owner of a sprawling home, and he serially pursued numerous fads and hobbies, some of which—mountain hiking and boating—were potentially quite dangerous. Rod Miller recalled the importance of that book and Rosenblatt's self-understanding of himself as Mr. Toad:

> One chapter Frank came to and he said, "This chapter's about me." And it's about Mr. Toad, who had wanted to get a bright shiny red motor car, and he was obsessed with this idea, and Frank identified with Mr. Toad, and he had many shiny red motor cars: projects. At the house, he'd get involved in interstellar communication, painting, sculpture, mountain climbing, and we'd all say, "Frank doesn't know anything about that," and two weeks later, Frank knew something about it, and two months later he knew an awful lot about it.[121]

Rosenblatt taught himself about boating and the basics of how to sail from reading, but he lacked extensive real-world experience, especially with a large boat like *Shearwater*. Shortly after purchasing it, Rosenblatt took several trips with others in the Long Island Sound, near City Island where he had purchased the boat, and down the East River. *Shearwater* spent the winter of 1970 in Maryland.

On his 43rd birthday jaunt, in 1971, Rosenblatt took along with him two young men for a sailing cruise across Maryland's Chesapeake Bay. They left from Oxford, located on the east side of the bay, and headed northwest, across the bay, toward An-

121 Rodman G. Miller, quoted in U.S. Congress, *Congressional Record*, 117th Congress, 21st session, July 28, 1971, H27717.

Fig. 2.15. Frank Rosenblatt and *Shearwater*. Image courtesy of William Mutch.

napolis. One of the young men accompanying Rosenblatt on the *Shearwater* that day was Walter Craig Johnsen, an undergraduate at Cornell at the time. Johnsen, who became a businessman and corporate executive, would later establish an endowment at Cornell, the Frank Rosenblatt Faculty Fellow Endowment, to honor Rosenblatt. The other was William Mutch, one of the many previously mentioned young residents of Chateau Rosenblatt and an important source for this biography. Mutch, who was the most experienced sailor of the group, had previously sailed with Rosenblatt several times before on the *Shearwater* and he described in an interview how during the crossing, and as the result of a shift in wind causing an accidental jibe, Rosenblatt was swept overboard. He was, according to Mutch, caught up in the sheets.[122] Rosenblatt was pulled back aboard but could not be resuscitated.[123]

122 "Professor, Inventor of 'Perceptron': Frank Rosenblatt," *The Washington Post,* July 14, 1971.

123 William Mutch, Zoom interview with James E. Dobson, July 22, 2022.

Rosenblatt was recognized as an important enough figure to produce something of a public archive of his memorial. *The New York Times's* obituary, along with his poem "Courage" and several of the eulogies and remarks given during his memorial event, were read into and published in the *Congressional Record.* The memorial event itself was held at Cornell shortly after his death, on July 16th. The memorial testimony was added to the *Congressional Record* on July 28th by Hugh L. Carey, a Democrat, who was at the time representing New York's 15th District. Carey introduced Rosenblatt to the members of Congress by calling him "a most gifted human being" and remarking on the tragedy of his early death. While noting his scientific achievements, Carey shared that Rosenblatt was primarily a gifted teacher and an inspiring leader:

> Dr. Frank Rosenblatt's spirit will, I hope, endure through others who will be inspired to follow in his footsteps, because throughout his life he gave freely and generously to young people who were in his classes and in his company and, in fact, he made his life a total inspiration to the young people around him.

It was not just Rosenblatt's success as a teacher or researcher or even his work on Senator Eugene McCarthy's presidential campaign that made him worthy of the honor of having his life presented to Congress, but also the government service of Maurice Rosenblatt. Maurice's longtime friendship with politicians included US Senators Eugene McCarthy and Gaylord Nelson; Carey includes several highly favorable comments on Maurice Rosenblatt's lobbying work by way of extending his condolences to Maurice's Washington colleagues.

The *Congressional Record* also contains eulogizing remarks from two campus leaders who had religious ties. Father David Connor recalled Rosenblatt's political activism on campus and throughout New England. Connor's comments were not religious in nature, as he had left the priesthood at this point, but were directed towards Rosenblatt's actions during the period that Connor termed the "crisis" of 1967–1971.[124] Connor also read Rosenblatt's poem "Courage" at the memorial. Cornell's Rabbi Morris Goldfarb provided religious sentiment for the occasion, quoting fragments from Ecclesiasticus:

> Fear not death, we are all destined to die; we share it with all who ever lived, with all who ever will be; bewail the dead, hide not your grief, do not restrain your mourning, but remember that continuing sorrow is worse than death; when the dead are adrift let their memory rest and be consoled when the soul departs; seek not to understand what is too difficult for you; search not for what is hidden from you; be not over-occupied with what is beyond you: you have been shown more than you can understand; as a drop of water in the sea, as a grain of sand on the shore, are man's few days in eternity; the good things in life last for limited days, but a good name endures forever.[125]

Rosenblatt was buried in the Quick Cemetery in Brooktondale, New York, not far from his home at Chateau Rosenblatt and the university at which he spent almost the entirety of his adult life. A metal plaque mounted to a large rock in the cemetery bears the inscription: "Frank Rosenblatt July 11, 1928–1971."

In 1973 the Frank Rosenblatt Memorial Reading Room was formally dedicated. The room was created through an endowment, with funds initially provided by Richard D. O'Brien, at that time director of the Division of Biological Sciences, and Frank Rosenblatt's brother Maurice. This space, housed in Room 155 in Langmuir Laboratory, contained material from Rosenb-

124 David Connor, quoted in Bill Chaisson, "We Won't Go – Nearly 50 Years after Anti-war Demonstrations Rocked Cornell, Members of Student Activist Groups to Return," *Ithaca Times*, November 5, 2014, https://www.ithaca.com/news/we-wont-go-nearly-50-years-after-anti-war-demonstrations-rocked-cornell-members-of-student/article_db7d4dae-6505-11e4-86a3-47b52dda7df2.html.

125 Morris Goldfarb, quoted in U.S. Congress, *Congressional Record*, 117th Congress, 21st session, July 28, 1971, H27718.

latt's professional library. There was also a charcoal portrait of Rosenblatt created by a Cornell University colleague, Hans Peter Kahn. At the moment of the library's dedication, Rosenblatt was remembered fondly by his colleagues and students; memories of him and his research in the larger scientific community did not last as long, his legacy covered over both by the AI Winter and the public's reception of him and his research. Langmuir Laboratory, an off-campus complex that had been purchased by Cornell in 1969 and used to house several scientific departments and central computing resources, was Rosenblatt's and the CSRP's intellectual home at the time of his death. By 1987, Langmuir Laboratory was no longer housed with any university departments or staff and today has become part of the Cornell Business & Technology Park. Kahn's charcoal portrait of Rosenblatt has been relocated to the third floor of Seeley G. Mudd Hall, and while the Frank Rosenblatt Memorial Reading Room unfortunately no longer exists as it was originally intended, Rosenblatt's legacy can be found elsewhere.

* * *

The many recent achievements of contemporary deep learning and the artificial intelligence applications of today (such as ChatGPT) originate in Rosenblatt's groundbreaking mid-twentieth century research. The widespread use of what are now explicitly referred to as Multi-Layer Perceptrons in the architecture of today's latest transformer networks powering Large Language Models (LLMs) and AI applications provide ample evidence that he was indeed heading on the right track. Rosenblatt anticipated the uses of generative AI as early as 1958. He imagined that the scientific and everyday problems that seemed unsurmountable in the 1950s would be solved by neural networks inspired by the design of his Perceptron. A neural network that began from nothing, from no knowledge about the world, and from empty values, would come to learn to complete many different tasks without explicit training. Such a network, Rosenblatt proposed, could combine different modalities of input, no longer separated into a photo or phono-perceptron, but a single system that could interact with images, with text, and with voice:

> In principle, it could read both print and script and could respond to verbal commands as well. The possibility also exists that it could automatically translate words spoken in one language into written or spoken words in another language. Eventually, the coupling of a perceptron with a conventional digital computer might carry us over the remaining obstacles of grammar and syntax. In the distant future, automatic navigation and landing systems, automatic pilots, and various recognition systems might make use of the perceptron. The application of such a system to library research and data gathering for scientific purposes is also a possibility.[126]

Like the functions of OpenAI's ChatGPT, Rosenblatt imagined that his Perceptron would make use of different modes of inputs with an easy-to-use interface. Such a device would have far-reaching impacts and profoundly alter the conditions of knowledge production. While Rosenblatt imagined that the coupling of a device with a computer would make this possible, what he saw as a limitation — the simulation of neural networks with a computer — has enabled this revolution. Today's LLMs are sophisticated and incredibly large Perceptrons. They are the brilliant offspring of a neural network first designed and simulated in 1958. The ability to run these models alongside chat applications has transformed artificial intelligence from science fiction to an everyday encounter. Rosenblatt's dreams for these devices live in the recent successes of contemporary artificial intelligence, even while AI research continues to struggle. Nevertheless, Rosenblatt's vision and approach have been vindicated. We see signs of this everywhere, from every time a "smart" car recognizes another vehicle in the road and automatically brakes

126 Frank Rosenblatt, "Design of an Intelligent Automaton," *Research Reviews* (Office of Naval Research, 1958), 13.

to the instant translation of a speaker from one language to another. The distant future imagined by Rosenblatt was sooner than he lived to realize, in part due to his engineering skills, his visionary insight, and his infectious enthusiasm. Any history of the achievements of modern AI that doesn't include him is not just faulty, but impoverished.

Notes on the Poems

The source material for the first three poems and the subsequent text chunk comes from the question and answers of a talk given by Frank Rosenblatt at the "Self-Organizing Systems" conference. Frank Rosenblatt, "Perceptual Generalization Over Transformation Groups," in *Self-Organizing Systems: Proceedings of an Interdisciplinary Conference*, ed. Marshall C. Yovits and Scott Cameron (Pergamon Press, 1960), 63–100, at 97.

"Brilliant Offspring": The source material for this erasure poem comes from an article summarizing a meeting with Rosenblatt and several *New Yorker* writers: Harding Mason, D. Stewart, and Brendan Gill, "Rival," *The New Yorker*, December 6, 1958, 44–45.

"New Navy Device Learns by Doing": This erasure poem takes an article by the same name, published in *The New York Times* on July 8, 1958, as the source material.

"Device Expected to 'Think'": This erasure poem takes an article by the same name, written by Herbert B. Nichols and published in *The Christian Science Monitor* on July 9, 1958, as the source material.

"Shades of Frankenstein!": This erasure poem takes "Navy's Going to Build a Robot That Can Think," published in the *Daily Boston Globe* on July 7, 1958, as its source material.

"For Machines": The source material for this erasure poem is an article titled "Electronic 'Brain' With Ability to Learn Now Being Built," written by Edward Gamarekian and published in *The Washington Post* on July 8, 1958.

"The Automation of Photointerpretation (using a 3x3 pixel matrix)": The source material for this erasure poem is a lab report: Albert E. Murray, "Perceptron Applicability to Photointerpretation," Phase 1 report for Project PICS, Report VE-1446G-1 (Cornell Aeronautical Laboratory, 1960).

"B.F. Skinner's Questions": This poem takes its epigraph from B.F. Skinner's book *About Behaviorism* (Vintage Books, 1976). The poem itself is made from the digital deformation of the language found in the book's epigraph.

The three poems titled "Frank Rosenblatt" are erasure poems that take the Cornell University Faculty Memorial Statement as the source text. The full text of the Cornell University Faculty Memorial Statement can be found here: https://ecommons.cornell.edu/bitstream/handle/1813/18965/Rosenblatt_Frank_1971.pdf.

"Unfashionable Machines": This poem is written in the perceptron form and uses lines from the Cornell University Faculty Memorial Statement (see above) and Léon Bottou's 2017 foreword to a reissue of Marvin L. Minsky and Seymour A. Papert's second edition of *Perceptrons* (MIT Press, 1972). The authors' handwritten alteration, "In Memory of Frank Rosenblatt," is the first "weight statement" in this poem.

"A Promising Line of Research": This poem uses Léon Bottou's foreword to the expanded, revised edition of Marvin L. Minsky and Seymour A. Papert's *Perceptrons* (MIT Press, 1988) and Frank Rosenblatt's obituary published in *The New York Times* on July 13, 1971.

"Principles of Neurodynamics vs. Perceptrons 0.0" through "Principles of Neurodynamics vs. Perceptrons 0.5" use Marvin L. Minsky and Seymour A. Papert's *Perceptrons,* rev. ed. (MIT Press, 1988) and Frank Rosenblatt's *Principles of Neurodynamics: Perceptrons and the Theory of Brain* (Spartan Books, 1962) as their source texts.

"Frank and Rod Visit Morocco": This series of poems makes use of three photographs of Rod Miller from the film in Frank Rosenblatt's camera, courtesy of William Mutch. The repeated phrase, "Frank was in love with my brother Rod," comes from an interview conducted with a member of the Miller family.

"Frank in Spain": This poem makes use of a photograph of Frank Rosenblatt from film in his own camera, developed after he died. Photo used courtesy of William Mutch.

Bibliography

Air War Study Group. *The Air War in Indochina*. Edited by Raphael Littauer and Norman Uphoff. Revised Edition. Beacon Press, 1972.

Beizer, Michael. "Restoring Courage to Jewish Hearts: Frank Rosenblatt's Mission in Siberia in 1919." *East European Jewish Affairs* 39, no. 1 (2009): 35–56. DOI: 10.1080/13501670902750279.

Borsellino, Antonio, and Augusto Gamba. "An Outline of a Mathematical Theory of PAPA." *Il Nuovo Cimento* 20, Suppl. 2 (1961): 221–31. DOI: 10.1007/BF02822644.

Bradway, Tyler, and Elizabeth Freeman, eds. *Queer Kinship: Race, Sex, Belonging, Form*. Duke University Press, 2022.

Brain, Alfred E., George Forsen, David Hall, and Charles Rosen. "A Large, Self-Contained Learning Machine." In *Proceedings of the Western Electronic Show and Convention*. IEEE, 1963.

Bridger, Sarah. *Scientists at War: The Ethics of Cold War Weapons Research*. Harvard University Press, 2015.

Bronfenbrenner, Urie, Thomas A. Ryan, and James J. Gibson. "Robert Brodie MacLeod." In *Memorial Statements of the Cornell University Faculty (1868–2009)*, edited by J. Robert

Cooke. *Cornell eCommons,* 2010. https://hdl.handle.net/1813/19318.

Chaisson, Bill. "We Won't Go – Nearly 50 Years After Anti-War Demonstrations Rocked Cornell, Members of Student Activist Groups to Return." *Ithaca Times,* November 5, 2014. https://www.ithaca.com/news/we-wont-go-nearly-50-years-after-anti-war-demonstrations-rocked-cornell-members-of-student/article_db7d4dae-6505-11e4-86a3-47b52dda7df2.html.

"C.U. Anti-War Group Lobbying in D.C." *Cornell Chronicle* 1, no. 30 (May 14, 1970).

Dobson, James E. "Early Machine Learning and Artificial Animal Intelligences." *Journal of the Midwest Modern Language Association* 57, no. 1 (2024): 63–89. DOI: 10.1353/mml.2024.a968076.

———. "On Reading and Interpreting Black Box Deep Neural Networks." *International Journal of Digital Humanities* 5 (2023): 431–49. DOI: 10.1007/s42803-023-00075-w.

———. "On the Confusion Matrix." *Configurations* 32, no. 4 (2024): 331–50. DOI: 10.1353/con.2024.a942087.

———. *The Birth of Computer Vision.* University of Minnesota Press, 2023.

Edwards, Paul N. *The Closed World: Computers and the Politics of Discourse in Cold War America.* MIT Press, 1997.

Emlen, Stephen T., Howard C. Howland, and Richard D. O'Brien. "Frank Rosenblatt." In *Memorial Statements of the Cornell University Faculty (1868–2009),* edited by J. Robert Cooke. *Cornell eCommons,* 2010. https://hdl.handle.net/1813/19318.

Fischler Martin A., and Oscar Firschein. *Intelligence: The Eye, the Brain, and the Computer.* Addison-Wesley, 1987.

Fisher, Ronald A. "The Use of Multiple Measurements in Taxonomic Problems." *Annals of Eugenics* 7, no. 2 (1936): 179–88. DOI: 10.1111/j.1469-1809.1936.tb02137.x.

Gamarekian, Edward. "Electronic 'Brain' With Ability to Learn Now Being Built." *The Washington Post,* July 8, 1958.

Gamba, Augusto. "The Papistor: An Optical PAPA Device." *Il Nuovo Cimento* 26, Suppl. 3 (1962): 371–73. DOI: 10.1007/BF02782173.

Gibson, James J., Paul Olum, and Frank Rosenblatt. "Parallax and Perspective During Aircraft Landings." *The American Journal of Psychology* 68, no. 3 (1955): 372–85. DOI: 10.2307/1418521.

Goldsmith, Samuel A. "Dr. Frank F. Rosenblatt." *The Jewish Social Service Quarterly* 4, no. 2 (1927): 117–19.

Haigh, Thomas, Mark Priestly, and Crispin Rope. *ENIAC in Action: Making and Remaking the Modern Computer.* MIT Press, 2016.

Halpern, Orit. "The Future Will Not Be Calculated: Neural Nets, Neoliberalism, and Reactionary Politics." *Critical Inquiry* 48, no. 2 (2022): 334–59. DOI: 10.1086/717313.

Haugeland, John. *Artificial Intelligence: The Very Idea.* MIT Press, 1985.

Hay, John C., Ben E. Lynch, and David R. Smith. "MARK I Perceptron Operators' Manual (Project PARA)." Report VG-1196-G-5. Cornell Aeronautical Laboratory, 1960.

Hayes, Donald P., Robin M. Williams, Jr., and Bruce P. Halpern. "William W. Lambert." In *Memorial Statements of the Cornell University Faculty (1868–2009),* edited by J. Robert Cooke. *Cornell eCommons,* 2010. https://hdl.handle.net/1813/19318.

Hebb, Donald O. *The Organization of Behavior: A Neuropsychological Theory.* 1949; repr. Taylor & Francis, 2002.

Hu, Jane. "Between Us: A Queer Theorist's Devoted Husband and Enduring Legacy." *The New Yorker,* December 9, 2015. https://www.newyorker.com/books/page-turner/between-us-a-queer-theorists-devoted-husband-and-enduring-legacy.

Hubel, David, and Torsten Wiesel. "Receptive Fields, Binocular Interaction and Functional Architecture in the Cat's Visual Cortex." *The Journal of Physiology* 160, no. 1 (1962): 106–54. DOI: 10.1113/jphysiol.1962.sp006837.

Huffman, Deborah. "Faculty Confrontation: Vote on CAL Expected Today." *Cornell Daily Sun,* October 11, 1967.
Irwin, Julia A. "Artificial Worlds and Perceptronic Objects: The CIA's Mid-Century Automatic Target Recognition." *Grey Room* 97 (2024): 6–35. DOI: 10.1162/grey_a_00415.
Kesler, Carl, and Frank Rosenblatt. "Further Simulation Experiments on Series-Coupled Perceptrons." In *Collected Technical Papers,* Volume 2, Report No. 5: Cognitive Systems Research Program, edited by Frank Rosenblatt. Cornell University, 1963.
Kotulak, Ronald. "New Machine Will Type Out What it 'Hears': Can Fill Secretary's Job, Expert Says." *Chicago Tribune,* June 18, 1963.
Leslie, Stuart W. *The Cold War and American Science: The Military-Industrial-Academic Complex at MIT and Stanford.* Columbia University Press, 1994.
Lettvin, Jerome, Humberto R. Maturana, Warren S. McCulloch, and Walter H. Pitts. "What the Frog's Eye Tells the Frog's Brain." *Proceedings of the IRE* 47, no. 11 (1959): 1940–51. DOI: 10.1109/JRPROC.1959.287207.
Mason, Harding, D. Stewart, and Brendan Gill. "Rival." *The New Yorker,* December 6, 1958, 44–45. https://www.newyorker.com/magazine/1958/12/06/rival-2.
Meyerhoff, T., Sarah McCarry, and Hal Sedgwick. "Life of Eve Kosofsky Sedgwick." *Eve Kosofsky Sedgwick.* https://evekosofskysedgwick.net/biography/biography.html.
McCorduck, Pamela. *Machines Who Think: A Personal Inquiry into the History and Prospects of Artificial Intelligence.* Second Edition. AK Peters, 2004.
McCulloch, Warren S., and Walter S. Pitts. "A Logical Calculus of the Ideas Immanent in Nervous Activity." *Bulletin of Mathematical Biophysics* 5 (1943): 115–33. DOI: 10.1007/BF02478259.
Minsky, Marvin. "Steps Toward Artificial Intelligence." *Proceedings of the IRE* 49, no. 1 (1961): 8–30. DOI: 10.1109/JRPROC.1961.287775.

———. "Theory of Neural-Analog Reinforcement Systems and its Application to the Brain-Model Problem." PhD diss., Princeton University, 1954.

Minsky, Marvin, and Seymour Papert. *Perceptrons*. MIT Press, 1969.

———. *Perceptrons*. Revised Edition. MIT Press, 1988.

Moon, Michael, Eve Kosofsky Sedgwick, Benjamin Gianni, and Scott Weir. "Queers in (Single-Family) Space." *Assemblage* 24 (1994): 30–37. DOI: 10.2307/3171189.

Murray, Albert E. "Perceptron Applicability to Photointerpretation." Phase 1 Report for Project PICS, Report VE-1446G-1. Cornell Aeronautical Laboratory, 1960.

———. "Perceptron Applications in Photo Interpretation." *Photogrammetric Engineering* 27, no. 4 (1961): 627–37.

"Navy's Going to Build Robot That Can Think." *Daily Boston Globe*, July 8, 1958.

"New Navy Device Learns by Doing: Psychologist Shows Embryo of Computer Designed to Read and Grow Wiser." *The New York Times*, July 8, 1958, 25. https://www.nytimes.com/1958/07/08/archives/new-navy-device-learns-by-doing-psychologist-shows-embryo-of.html.

Nichols, Herbert B. "Device Expected to 'Think.'" *The Christian Science Monitor*, July 9, 1958.

Olazaran, Mikel. "A Sociological Study of the Official History of the Perceptrons Controversy." *Social Studies of Science* 26, no. 3 (1996): 611–59. DOI: 10.1177/030631296026003005.

Pasquinelli, Matteo. *The Eye of the Master: A Social History of Artificial Intelligence*. Verso, 2023.

Paszke, Adam, Sam Gross, Francisco Massa, Adam Lerer, James Bradbury, Gregory Chanan, Trevor Killeen, Zeming Lin, Natalia Gimelshein, Luca Antiga, Alban Desmaison, Andreas Köpf, Edward Yang, Zach DeVito, Martin Raison, Alykhan Tejani, Sasank Chilamkurthy, Benoit Steiner, Lu Fang, Junjie Bai, and Soumith Chintala. "PyTorch: An Imperative Style, High-Performance Deep Learning Library." In *Advances in Neural Information Processing Systems (NeurIPS) 32*, edited by H. Larochelle, A.

Beygelzimer, F. d'Alché-Buc, E. Fox, and R. Garnett. Curran Associates, 2019.
"Professor, Inventor of 'Perceptron': Frank Rosenblatt." *The Washington Post,* July 14, 1971.
Redmond, Kent C., and Thomas M. Smith. *From Whirlwind to MITRE: The R&D Story of The SAGE Air Defense* Computer. MIT Press, 2000.
Roberts, Sam. "Faculty Reveals CIA Sessions." *Cornell Daily Sun,* March 8, 1967.
Robles-Anderson, Erica, and Scott Ferguson. "The Visual Cliff: Eleanor Gibson & The Origins of Affordance." *Money on the Left,* April 19, 2022. https://moneyontheleft.org/2022/04/19/the-visual-cliff-eleanor-gibson-the-origins-of-affordance/.
Rochester, N., J. Holland, L. Haibt, and W. Duda. "Tests on a Cell Assembly Theory of the Action of the Brain, Using a Large Digital Computer." *IEEE Transactions on Information Theory* 2, no. 3 (1956): 80–93. DOI: 10.1109/TIT.1956.1056810.
Rosenblatt, Frank. "Analytic Techniques for the Study of Neural Nets." *IEEE Transactions on Applications and Industry* 83, no. 74 (1964): 285–92. DOI: 10.1109/TAI.1964.5407758.
———. "Comparison of a Five-Layer Perceptron with Human Visual Performance." In *Natural Automata and Useful Simulations,* edited by H.H. Patee, E.A. Edelsack, Louis Fein, and A.B. Callahan. Spartan Books, 1963.
———. "Design of an Intelligent Automaton." In *Research Reviews.* Office of Naval Research, 1958.
———. "Final Summary Report on Contract Nor 401-40: Cognitive Systems Research Program." Office of Naval Research, March 1971. https://apps.dtic.mil/sti/pdfs/AD0720416.pdf.
———. "Perceptron Simulation Experiments." *Proceedings of the IRE* 48, no. 3 (1960): 301–9. DOI: 10.1109/JRPROC.1960.287598.
———. "Perceptron Simulation Experiments (Project Para)." Report No. VG-1196-6-3. Cornell Aeronautical Laboratory, June 1959. https://babel.hathitrust.org/cgi/pt?id=coo.31924004657973&seq=1.

———. "Perceptual Generalization Over Transformation Groups." In *Self-Organizing Systems: Proceedings of an Interdisciplinary Conference,* edited by Marshall C. Yovits and Scott Cameron. Pergamon Press, 1960.

———. *Principles of Neurodynamics: Perceptrons and the Theory of Brain Mechanisms.* Spartan Books, 1962.

———. "The *k*-Coefficient: Design and Trial Application of a New Technique for Multivariate Analysis." PhD diss., Cornell University, 1956.

———. "The Perceptron: A Perceiving and Recognizing Automaton (Project PARA)." Report No. 85-460-1. Cornell Aeronautical Laboratory, January 1957.

———. "The Perceptron: A Probabilistic Model for Information Storage and Organization in the Brain." *Psychological Review* 65, no. 6 (1958): 386–408. DOI: 10.1037/h0042519.

Rosenblatt, Frank, and Rodman G. Miller. "Behavioral Assay Procedures for Transfer of Learned Behavior by Brain Extracts." *Proceedings of the National Academy of Science* 56, no. 5 (1966): 1423–30. DOI: 10.1073/pnas.56.6.1683.

Rosenblatt, Frank F. *The Chartist Movement: In Its Social and Economic Aspects.* 1916; repr. Routledge, 2020.

Rumelhart, David E., Geoffrey E. Hinton, and Ronald J. Williams. "Learning Representations by Back-Propagating Errors." *Nature* 323 (1986): 533–36. DOI: 10.1038/323533a0.

Rumelhart, David E., and David Zipser. "Feature Discovery by Competitive Learning." *Cognitive Science* 9 (1985): 75–112. DOI: 10.1207/s15516709cog0901_5.

Scates, Shelby. *Maurice Rosenblatt and the Fall of Joseph McCarthy.* University of Washington Press, 2006.

Sedgwick, Eve Kosofsky. "A Death by Water (1969-1971)." In *Bathroom Songs: Eve Kosofsky Sedgwick as a Poet,* edited by Jason Edwards. punctum books, 2017. DOI: 10.21983/P3.0189.1.00.

———. *A Dialogue on Love.* Beacon Press, 1999.

———. "Tales of the Avunculate: Queer Tutelage in *The Importance of Being Earnest*." In Eve Kosofsky Sedgwick, *Tendencies*. Duke University Press, 1993.

———. *Tendencies*. Duke University Press, 1993.

———. *Touching Feeling: Affect, Pedagogy, Performativity*. Duke University Press, 2003.

Sedgwick, Eve Kosofsky, and Adam Frank. "Shame in the Cybernetic Fold: Reading Silvan Tomkins." In *Touching Feeling: Affect, Pedagogy, Performativity*, by Eve Kosofsky Sedgwick. Duke University Press, 2003.

Singh-Dhaliwal, Ranjodh, Théo Lepage-Richer, and Lucy Suchman, eds. *Neural Networks*. meson press, 2024. DOI: 10.14619/0832.

Skinner, B.F. *About Behaviorism*. Vintage Books, 1976.

Vaswani, Ashish, Noam Shazeer, Niki Parmar, Jakob Uszkoreit, Llion Jones, Aidan N. Gomez, Łukasz Kaiser, and Illia Polosukhin. "Attention Is All You Need." *Advances in Neural Information Processing Systems* 30 (2017). DOI: 10.48550/arXiv.1706.03762.

Werbos, Paul. "Backpropagation: Past and Future." *IEEE International Conference on Neural Networks* 1 (1988): 343–53.

Wilson, Elizabeth A. *Affect and Artificial Intelligence*. University of Washington Press, 2010.

Yovits, Marshall C., George T. Jacobi, and Gordon T. Goldstein, eds. *Self-Organizing Systems, 1962*. Spartan Books, 1962.

www.ingramcontent.com/pod-product-compliance
Lightning Source LLC
Chambersburg PA
CBHW072045160426
43197CB00014B/2642
9781685712167